"Insightful and access... essential guidebook on the path of libera..."
TARA BRACH, author of *Trusting the Gold*

"In the most recent installment of *Ancient Wisdom for Our Times* Lama Tsomo shares her experience with the deep practices of Tibetan Buddhism. She writes with clarity, humor and with practical support to guide us to a better and more fulfilled life. It feels like being given a gift to read *Deepening Wisdom, Deepening Connection* and an invitation to slow down to experience life."
SHARON SALZBERG, author of *Lovingkindness* and *Real Change*

"In today's divisive world, the ability to extend the boundaries of love and compassion beyond what we know requires courage and skill. In this book, Lama Tsomo brings us potent practices that help us cultivate what our minds and hearts know is true— allowing something beautiful to emerge from the challenge."
VAN JONES, CNN host and Dream Corps founder

"Writing from her lived experience of many years of Buddhist practice, Lama Tsomo delivers in her latest book *Deepening Wisdom, Deepening Connection*, the foundational elements of the Buddhist heart practices.

She continues to deliver her unique style of teaching with clarity, humor, and deep dharma, that reaches all hearts and minds and brings us face-to-face with who we really are as human beings and our highest possibilities."
KONDA MASON, Mindfulness Meditation teacher, co-founder/ president at Jubilee Justice, and host of *The Brown Rice Hour* podcast

"Lama Tsomo is a teacher for our time—as discord feels normalized, and humanity's blindness threatens life itself. I love her voice—full of compassion, humility, and deep wisdom. I love her method—artfully weaving a tapestry of life-changing concepts using stories, surprising scientific findings, her own life experiences . . . and even humor. What a gift to all of us seeking to grasp the true nature of existence."
FRANCES MOORE LAPPÉ, author or coauthor of 20 books, beginning with *Diet for a Small Planet*

TIBETAN BUDDHIST PRACTICE SERIES

Ancient Wisdom for Our Times

BOOK 3 *Deepening Wisdom,*
Deepening Connection

TIBETAN BUDDHIST PRACTICE SERIES

Ancient Wisdom
for Our Times

BOOK 3 *Deepening Wisdom,*
Deepening Connection

Lama Tsomo

foreword by HIS HOLINESS THE DALAI LAMA XIV

Namchak

Namchak

PUBLISHING

Namchak

PUBLISHING

*The Namchak Foundation supports the study and
practice of the Namchak Lineage of Tibetan Buddhism.*

Namchak.org

Cover design: Kate Basart/Union Pageworks
Book design: Mary Ann Casler & Kate Basart/Union Pageworks
Cover art from *The Encyclopedia of Tibetan Symbols and Motifs* by Robert Beer,
© 1999 by Robert Beer. Reprinted by arrangement with Shambhala
Publications, Inc., Boulder, CO. www.shambhala.com.
Editorial: Michael Frisbie
Copyeditor & Proofreader: Kristyn Asseff
Indexer: Michael Ferreira/Ferreira Indexing, Inc.
Printed in Hong Kong
Printed on FSC-certified materials

Library of Congress Control Number: 2021917053

ISBN: 978-1951096-00-7

First printing, 2022

27 26 25 24 23 22   1 2 3 4 5 6 7 8

Contents

Tulku Sangak Rinpoche, His Holiness the Dalai Lama XIV, Lama Tsomo

THE DALAI LAMA

FOREWORD

As our world becomes ever more connected, the world's great spiritual traditions are able to get to know each other better. This provides their followers opportunities to learn from one another and develop a deeper appreciation and respect for each other's teachings, traditions and practices. I, for one, have learned a great deal from the insights of spiritual traditions other than my own.

I often describe myself as a staunch Buddhist. However, I have never felt the urge to propagate Buddhism with the aim of converting others to my point of view. In general, I believe it's better and safer for most people to stay within the religious tradition of their birth. The world's faiths evolved in specific geographical and cultural circumstances, which gives them an affinity to the spiritual inclinations and needs of specific communities. I am quite open about this, especially when I am asked to speak about Buddhism in the West, where the main spiritual traditions are historically Judeo-Christian.

At the same time, I recognize that, especially in today's interconnected world, there will be individuals who find the approach of traditions other than those to which they were born to be more effective and suited to their own spiritual aspirations. I know many people in the West, in both North America and Europe, who engage in serious study and practice of Buddhist teachings. They find the advice for training the mind presented in the Buddhist teachings to be profoundly beneficial and meaningful. Some such Western Buddhists have been steadfast in their commitment to their Buddhist practice for several decades, demonstrating a deep dedication. It is in this context that I am happy to see the publication of this new book *A Westerner's Introduction and Guide to Tibetan Buddhism*. Written by Sangak Tsomo, a long-time student and practitioner of Tibetan Buddhism, the book outlines the basic views of the Tibetan tradition and examples of some of its practices for the interested modern reader. I am pleased to note that while the author describes her personal journey into Buddhism in some detail, she continues to honor her traditional Jewish heritage.

I have no doubt that Western readers who wish to deepen their understanding of Tibetan Buddhist practices will find much to interest them here, and that members of other faiths, or even those who have none, will enjoy this sincere account of spiritual exploration.

June 6, 2014

Pema Khandro Ling
1221 Luisa Street, Suite A
Santa Fe, NM 87505
santafe@ewam.org

Nyingma School of Tibetan Buddhism

Ewam Sang-ngag Ling
PO Box 330 Arlee, MT 59821
406.726.0217 • www.ewam.org
admin@ewam.org

Gochen Tulku Sang-ngag Rinpoche
Spiritual Director

Foreword

For the benefit of Westerners who are beginners in the practice of Buddhism, Lama Tsomo has drawn on her own knowledge of Western and Eastern ways of thinking and devoted all her efforts to writing this current work, in order to provide a bridge that will forge a connection between these cultures. I am delighted that she has completed this book, and offer my sincere and heartfelt thanks and best wishes to her in this endeavor.

On this note, let me say a few words about Lama Tsomo, the author of this book, since she is a personal student of mine. Beginning with our initial meeting in 1995, she undertook the study and practice of the Buddhist teachings, including her spending two or three months each year in strict retreat, in addition to maintaining an uninterrupted daily practice. In this way, she has dedicated herself enthusiastically to completing a system of training from the preliminary stages up to and including the advanced yogic disciplines (*tsa-lung*) and Dzogchen practices.

On the basis of her efforts, in 2005 I formally recognized Lama Tsomo's accomplishments in an investiture ceremony that took place in conjunction with the graduation of the nuns who participated in the three-year retreat program at my meditation center of Kusum Khandro Ling in Pharping, Nepal.

Following this, in 2006, on the occasion of the final year of the intensive study program at Ewam Sang-ngag Ling in Arlee, Montana, I conferred on Lama Tsomo the formal title of a lama of the Ewam Foundation.

She has now authored this book to introduce people to the Buddhist teachings, in order to help new practitioners on into the future. I encourage all to read and study this text with a sense of trust in its usefulness, and am sure that they will profit greatly through such efforts. Please take this advice to heart.

This was written in my retreat cabin by the teaching throne of Longchenpa at Ewam Pema Khandro Ling, by me, the sixth holder of the title of Gochen Tulku.

Sang-ngag Tenzin
April 2014

~ *Ewam Nepal* ~
Turquoise Leaf Nunnery - Phone: 977-1-710-094/Sang-ngag Phurba Ling Retreat Center - Phone: 977-1-710-093
POB 7032 Devi G.B.S. Pharping Kathmandu, Nepal

Ewam is a federally registered 501(c)(3) US non-profit organization

Welcome Back!

his third book is the next natural progression in the Tibetan Buddhist Practice Series *Ancient Wisdom for Our Times,* after the introductory book, *Why Bother?,* and the second, *Wisdom & Compassion (Starting With Yourself).* If you've read the earlier books and been doing the practices for a year or more, you're most likely ready for this one. I hope you've been studying and practicing with fellow journeyers, sharing with each other your questions and answers as you've been reading, doing the Happify track called "Hack Life's Challenges by Training Your Mind" and/or taking the eCourse, discussing challenges and victories as you establish your practice, do your practice, and test it all in the laboratory of your inner and outer life. Maybe most of all, I hope you've been going to in-person Shamata programs—either ours or with other Buddhist masters. I've found that doing all of the above, alone and with others, is extremely helpful and satisfying, in various ways. Perhaps you've found that too.

Of course, you may have come to *Deepening Wisdom, Deepening Connection* by your own path, rather than through this series. Either way, WELCOME! I've included a brief chart below to give you an idea of the foundation on which this book rests, in case you need to brush up or fill in any gaps. For example, if you happened to have learned Shamata from somewhere else but you haven't learned Tonglen, you might either want to get Book 2 of this series and look at that section, learn it from our online course at Namchak.org, or buy the book *Tonglen: The Path of Transformation* by Pema Chödrön. She's a true master and a great teacher of Tonglen and many other practices. Again, for more specifics on things I'll assume you know, see the chart below. I want you to feel like this is a comfortable and natural continuation and deepening in your practice.

> I want you to feel like this is a comfortable and natural continuation and deepening in your practice.

If you haven't read the first two books or haven't learned the practices in the second *(Wisdom & Compassion)* you might be a little lost. In fact, reading this tiny bit of this volume, you might already be feeling like it's unclear. If you haven't studied Buddhism in general before, or Clearing the Stale Energies (a.k.a. the Tibetan Nose Blow,) Shamata, and Tonglen, you'll be really lost. If you're just coming to meditation practice in general and/or Buddhist practice specifically, I'd suggest taking yourself on the adventures of Book 1 for some background (and lots of storytelling) and Book 2 for the three preceding practices before continuing with this book. It may seem like very delayed gratification, but I don't see it that way. Hopefully it's its *own* gratification! If you've learned some of the above practices and been doing them awhile, you might be ready to start here after all. For those of you somewhere in between, again, here is a chart so you can just read some particular chapter from Book 1 and/or 2, to catch up quickly.

Catch-Up Chart

CURRENT KNOWLEDGE/ EXPERIENCE	BEST TO READ FIRST
None	All of Books 1 & 2
Only Shamata	Books 1 & 2: Everything but the *Shamata* section.
Only Tonglen	Books 1 & 2: Everything but the *Tonglen* section
At least 6 months Tonglen and Shamata	Book 1: You might enjoy *Why the Buddha Bothered, Why Tulku Sangak Rinpoche Bothered, The Good News* Book 2: *Tibetan Nose Blow*
Tonglen, Shamata, Clearing the Stale Energies	Book 1: You might enjoy *Why Tulku Sangak Rinpoche Bothered, Tibetan Use of Imagery, The Good News* Book 2 or a short video from our website (Namchak.org): *Round Robin*

From here on, I'm going to assume you've read the first two books or the pieces you needed to, and been doing the practices regularly for at least six months. And if, at any point, you feel you need a refresher or reminder from the earlier books, please refresh yourself! Here we go!

Following spread: Elk tracks at Namchak Retreat Ranch

Statue from Stupa Garden at the Namchak Retreat Ranch with bison in background

Introduction

In *Why Bother?* and *Wisdom & Compassion*, the first two books of this series, we looked at how we got into this endlessly spinning dream of *Samsara*, and how we might begin to wake up from it. It sure worked for the Buddha! Remember, in Sanskrit the word *"buddha"* means "one who's awake." "Awake" was the simple way that the Buddha referred to himself, after he saw through the dream he'd formerly thought of as real life.

We talked about our *karma* ("action," in Sanskrit) and habits of mind sending us into the next dream—waking or otherwise—and our having very little freedom or say in the matter. So that's why Buddhists focus on "liberation." We Americans talk proudly of freedom, but often it feels like the "freedom" to be led around by the nose by our habit-motivated cravings and anxieties rather than our deepest, truest motivations. I want *real* freedom. That's why I do all this daily practice and retreat. I can *feel* the progress—and it feels good! And I also feel passionate about helping anyone else who wants real freedom—whoever happens to connect with this particular path.

We looked at the Four Noble Truths about our situation. I talked a lot about "suffering," but that's actually not a very accurate translation of the Sanskrit word *dukka*, which means something more like "insufficiency" or lack of real satisfaction—a sense that something's basically wrong. Dzigar Kongtrul Rinpoche, who is from Tibet but has spent a lot of time with Westerners, says that we Westerners have a particular twist on this idea of something being basically wrong or flawed. We think, "Something's wrong *with* ME." I say we think there's something wrong with both our circumstance and with ourselves.

Perhaps this comes from the Christian notion of Original Sin. Or maybe it was somewhere in the European folk soul. As a Jewish person, I suffer from the Jewish guilt we've heard so much about. Whatever the reason, I believe Dzigar Kongtrul Rinpoche has a point. And I agree with Rev. Matthew Fox and Meister Eckhart, among others, who speak of Original Blessing. As you might remember from Book 1, the Tibetans speak of Original Purity.* All the practices of Buddhism are about clearing away the flaws to reveal that true essence—much like clouds clearing away, revealing the sun that was there all along.

If we're inherently flawed—if that's our truest, deepest nature— there would be no basis for realizing buddhahood. If we clear away the clouds, only to reveal more clouds—or clean off the windshield only to find that it's irreparably defective in the first place—then our quest to reveal our original purity would be futile. I wonder if a lot of Westerners, believing that they're essentially flawed and therefore beyond liberation, struggle and struggle with Buddhist practices for years, not sure why they're stalled. But how could their efforts succeed if they believe there's no fundamental purity to be revealed? What a frustrating setup! Please look deep into your mind as you practice, to

---

* Interestingly, some Jewish scholars also use this term. Rabbi Stuart Federow writes, "Jews believe that one is born into the world with original purity, not original sin." (Source: see page 167.)

Apple orchard at the main permaculture planting, Namchak Retreat Ranch

see if you glimpse such a view of yourself—probably unconscious, way in the background. But it's all the more dangerous if you can't pull it out front and examine it.

As you sit in Shamata, you're in a perfect position to catch such thoughts "in the act" and begin to see them for what they are. Shamata also helps you directly experience your true essential nature. As a child, and beyond, you might have unconsciously absorbed the "fatal flaw" view of human nature (and therefore *your* essential nature) from those around you. Now you have a chance to see what you are—what we all are—really made of.

As a psychotherapist, the deeper I went into these practices, the more I was able to see my own pure essence, the more I was able to see it in my clients. You probably won't be surprised to know they responded strongly to that! My very seeing and focusing on their purer selves was like a grow light: they blossomed. It seemed to me that the therapy tools I'd learned were only about fifteen percent of the equation, and the rest was this "secret sauce." Imagine if we all saw each other that way. How about ourselves?

In Tonglen, as well as other practices in this book, we *begin* with love and compassion for ourselves. These practices, sometimes working with image and breath, bring that deep experience again and again, to retrain us to a more natural way of thinking: that we are a "child of God," a wave on the ocean and therefore made of that pure water.

I can also see how many could benefit from working with a good psychotherapist. I sure have! Western psychology gets at our gross personality flaws in particular ways that can dovetail nicely with meditation practice. (Because I'm a trained psychotherapist and a Buddhist lama—an interdisciplinary/cross-platform twofer—I truly appreciate the synergistic benefits of these two approaches.) I hasten to add that each of those two paths/disciplines needs to be practiced intact; on its own terms. Mixing them into mish-mash—psychobabble/pseudo-*Dharma* mush—renders both useless or worse.

Icefog at the Namchak Retreat Ranch

You and your therapist might diverge on the issue of whether we're all innately flawed ("original neuroses" instead of Original Sin, perhaps), but remember that until we reach enlightenment and are liberated from Samsara, we *are* all dealing with our own neuroses, barriers, and blind spots. The question isn't whether we're neurotic, because we are. The question is whether our essential nature is our neuroses, which it isn't. That's a key distinction. It feels quite a bit different to see yourself as essentially pure but with confusion and bad habits covering that over, rather than essentially flawed. Actually, if your therapist thinks you're *innately* flawed, I suggest finding a new therapist.

In the second book, you learned Shamata and Tonglen practices. As I mentioned there, they balance each other nicely. Tonglen is a training in compassion, practiced by all branches of Tibetan Buddhism, and similar practices are common to all of Buddhism. As I mentioned above, many Westerners find it deeply healing to begin Tonglen sessions by practicing compassion for themselves. But compassion is just one of the Four Boundless Qualities: Compassion, Loving Kindness, Sympathetic Joy, and Equanimity.* In your Round Robin practice, you can use any of those Four to get you to the place of feeling how you're not alone, but deeply connected to others, in ever-widening circles. Remember the Buddhist teaching that the root of Samsara is the illusion that we're separate from each other. So the Four Boundless Qualities practices help us to get at that root, not just to understand conceptually, but to *feel*, to *experience* how we're not separate.

In this book we'll fold those into our Round Robin practice so that we have three more avenues to that deep, heartfelt connection—to the way things really are. Then with *Vipassana* (literally "Sublime Seeing," in Sanskrit) we'll actually get to use our analytical minds . . . to get past them. It will be another avenue of finding our way to clearly *seeing* the true nature of ourselves and creation.

So let's begin with those practices that are still common to all Buddhist traditions: the Four Boundless Qualities (a.k.a. Four Immeasurables).

---

* If you've studied in the Theravada tradition you would know these as the Four Bramaviharas, literally the Four Abodes of Brahma, or the Four Sublime Attitudes.

Section One

THE FOUR BOUNDLESS QUALITIES

Loving Kindness
Compassion
Sympathetic Joy
Equanimity

Guan Yin at the Garden of One Thousand Buddhas

CULTIVATING BODHICITTA

Bodhicitta means "mind of awakening." "Buddha" and "Bodhi" are different forms of the Sanskrit word for "awake." For a very, very long time we've been dreaming that we're a wave that's separate from the ocean. While we can point to an individual wave and observe its unique shape, it's of course not really separate/ divorced from the ocean. But we've seen it in this confused way for so long that the habit is deeply set. We believe that this illusion of separateness is the way things really are. As we try to wake up out of this dream of being our own separate wave, we can apply practices from two basic angles—*seeing* how we're not separate and *feeling* how we're not separate.

Through Shamata (Tranquil Abiding) we begin to *see* the empty (non-concrete) essence of all things. We experience a quality of that empty essence—awareness. This experience, our recognition, is wisdom. As we experience this empty (non-substantial), aware essence, we also come to then *feel* another of its qualities—the warmth of compassion.

But we can get there another way, almost the opposite sequence: starting with *feeling* how we're joined at the root, landing in that great ocean we've spoken of, and then *seeing*, recognizing, how we're not separate.

Sometimes we're motivated by curiosity, by wanting to understand how it all works, so it makes sense to move from wisdom to loving compassion. Sometimes we're motivated by pain. Sometimes that pain comes from something happening in our lives that we don't want, something we're trying to avoid; sometimes the pain springs from grasping at something we want but never seem to be able to have, or have enough of, or hold onto long enough. In any of these circumstances, we may begin with our own feelings, extending outward to others who might also be feeling something similar. We've experienced that in Tonglen, widening our view so we can begin to clearly see the whole ocean.

Mother Teresa, who worked with the most desperately impoverished in India, said that Westerners suffer from poverty of the heart"—spiritual poverty and loneliness. We don't have many places to turn to, so many of us seek to assuage that loneliness and spiritual vacuum through romantic love. Yet half of the US marriages end in divorce, and that's not counting all the long-term, non-married relationships that end, or marriages that continue but very unhappily. I think we might do well to follow the advice of American songwriter David Wilcox, in his beautiful song, "Break in the Cup," about a couple who can't fulfill each other's needs or fill each other's emptiness because each has a "break in the cup," causing the love to leak out. At the end of the song, he invites his beloved to go with him "to the waterfall."

What exactly is the waterfall? How do we find our way there? Years ago, I felt deeply impoverished in both the spiritual and love departments. It seems I was typically American in that way. Typically human, perhaps? I'm sharing all of these methods and insights with you because they have led me to the waterfall. This wave found its way to the ocean . . . where it was all along. Of course I still spend plenty of time lost in my dream of reality, but at least I'm better at changing channels now—tuning in to the deeper reality. If you're suffering from these impoverishments, I'm hoping you can use these methods (if these are the ones for you) to get you there too. The particular practices in this book, the Four Boundless Qualities, are among the quickest, most direct ways to begin to taste the waterfall—which is still a bit upstream, at first, but already starting to quench our thirst. Perhaps you already have a sense of that from Tonglen. Little wonder—it's the most common way to practice one of the four: Boundless Compassion.

I believe the waterfall Wilcox is referring to is the source of all—the place where we join, the great ocean that we've been speaking of. Remember, wisdom and compassion are both essential qualities of the great ocean of awareness that is our source. They work together, two routes to the same place. The route that cultivates these buddha qualities of profound connection through the heart is bodhicitta. We're not trying to manufacture Buddha Nature as we cultivate these four qualities; we're creating experiences through which we can wake up to the deep connection that's always there.

Besides the pair of seeing and feeling our common source, Buddhism offers us another pair: these practices are always either *clearing away* obscurations, or *bringing forth* our buddha qualities (qualities of our

true essence). In Shamata we're mainly clearing away obscurations—splatters, warping, etc., of our windshields. In Bodhicitta training, we're bringing forth and maturing our innate Buddha Nature—in this case, the Four Boundless Qualities: Loving Kindness (usually written "Lovingkindness"), Compassion, Sympathetic Joy, and Equanimity.

We have already begun cultivating bodhicitta through Tonglen. Tonglen, along with the other three Boundless Qualities, is in the category of Aspirational Bodhicitta: we're training our capacity, and making heartful aspirations for the well-being of others. The second category is Engaged Bodhicitta, which is about doing something when you get off the cushion. We use Tonglen to train in compassion, ever deepening our capacity for compassion and expanding the scope. We can train in bodhicitta in other ways too. In Buddhism the classic way is to train in the Four Boundless (a.k.a. Immeasurable) Qualities. Again, it's 1) Boundless Loving Kindness, 2) Boundless Compassion, 3) Boundless Sympathetic Joy, and 4) Boundless Equanimity.

I'll let you in on a little secret. All four of these practices are avenues to one goal: feeling deeply and affectionately connected to all and everyone. We already feel closely connected to the ones we love—for example, those we call "my dog," "my cat," "my child," "my best friend." Notice what those terms all have in common. Yes, that first cousin of "I" ("ego" in Latin): "my." So even though we feel love, compassion, and sympathetic joy, it's limited to our favorite people and critters. Do we feel those things just as strongly for people and other creatures we don't know? And how about people who have caused us problems? These four practices are called "Boundless" because, through regular practice, we can expand our circle of loving connection to include *everybody*—eventually even people who drive us crazy! Honest!

> I'll let you in on a little secret. All four of these practices are avenues to one goal: feeling deeply and affectionately connected to all and everyone.

Why go through the effort of stretching such caring to the guy we passed on the street, or worse yet, someone we don't like? Because it's a direct antidote to loneliness, for one thing. For another, it's a great antidote to that famous, ultimate troublemaker: ego identification. Our habit (and it is only a habit) of thinking the world revolves around us is out of sync with the way things actually work. No wonder, then, that it makes for so much misery!

This means that in order to experience those three in a "Boundless" way—Love, Compassion, and Sympathetic Joy—we'll need to practice Boundless Equanimity. I'll let you in on another secret: you've already started. You've been combining Boundless Equanimity with compassion in order to make it Boundless Compassion whenever you've been doing Tonglen. And it's one of these Four Boundless practices. And you thought you were starting something totally new!

Let's now take a look from 35,000 feet at these Four Boundless Qualities, starting with Loving Kindness. By Loving Kindness, we mean simply our love for others—like the love that parents feel for their children. An example often used is mother and/or father birds (depending on the species) who, despite the hardship, build a nice nest, sitting, warming the eggs for weeks, then work very hard to find food for their babies, even risking their own lives to save them from predators. The avian parents treat their babies with love, protectiveness, and affection. In Buddhism the goal is "Boundless" Kindness though, because we don't want to practice just in the preferential way that a mother or father bird (or human) does—lavishing that strong a love only on their own babies.

That last point is key to getting these practices right. As we've seen, they're designed to help get us past seeing ourselves as this tiny, separate entity—cut off from everything and everyone. If we're to use Boundless Loving Kindness to find our way back to everyone through our loving hearts, then we need to expand the practice, ring by concentric ring, as we did with Tonglen, eventually including all.

The second one, Boundless Compassion (which, as we've said, is pursued through the practice of Tonglen,) is our fervent need to stop the suffering of another. If we feel deep Loving Kindness for another, then when they suffer, we can't bear to see it. We all know that feeling of desperately wanting to ease the suffering of someone dear to us, whether or not we have the means to do so.

As you remember, with Tonglen we start with ourselves, then those we feel close to, then expand our circle of compassion until all people—all creatures—are within it. The idea is to eventually expand our wish to ease suffering beyond just those we already know and love. We want to extend it to absolutely all beings.

But what if something *good* is happening to somebody? Don't we still care about them? Yes: the third Boundless Quality is Sympathetic Joy—in other words, feeling happy for someone else's happiness. If your friend just got a job they really wanted and they're jumping up and down with joy, you want to jump up and down with them. In a simple, everyday moment, when someone smiles, we often can't keep ourselves from smiling. Again, the idea is to expand the ring of Sympathetic Joy to include those we don't know—or maybe even those whose happiness piques our envy.

One of these men just won the 1976 Wimbledon championship. Can you tell which? The guy on the left is Ilie Năstase who, at thirty years old, was nearing the end of his career. They say his nickname was "Nasty" because, well, his temper was. The guy on the right is Björn

Borg who, at twenty years old, was at the beginning of what later turned out to be a stellar career. Okay, now I'll tell you in case you hadn't already guessed: Năstase lost to Borg. What a noble, beautiful example of Sympathetic Joy.

The last one is Boundless Equanimity, sometimes referred to as Impartiality. I want to stress again, that without this one in play, none of the others will be very "Boundless." The boundary will stop with those we care about: *my* family, *my* friends, *my* political party, *my* country. If we practice preference, we're serving our ego. We've already tried that plenty, and it hasn't worked well for us. So practicing the other three without this one will actually make the ego habit worse. Seriously, you'd be better off not practicing at all! Instead we're trying to loosen our desperate grip on ego, *by reaching past our ego and joining with others, through our natural Bodhicitta motivation.*

We all experience these qualities already. When you saw that picture of the tennis champions your heart was no doubt moved—Sympathetic Joy for *them!* That's your true nature shining through, between the clouds of ego-clinging habit. Right now we have both the sun and the clouds. The thing we have in our favor is that the clouds quickly pass by. They're not our true nature. Our confusion about how things really are—and the habits stemming from this confusion—can be cleared away, and our essential nature will remain. New habits stemming from our essential nature can replace them. As with any habits, at first we have to focus on a new way of thinking and doing things again and again. As time goes on, the new habits take on their own momentum. Luckily, in this case they've got the power of our true nature behind them.

Our own innate buddha qualities, like Loving Kindness, inspire us to *want* to loosen our grip in order to join with everyone in these four ways, so all we have to do is enhance that natural tendency.

If Only I Could Stop Thinking "If Only . . . "

One obstacle to our own happiness, and to our ability to meaningfully care for others, can be a reluctance to accept circumstances, things, and people as they are. We cling not only to our illusory vision of what is "real" but to our desires to tweak the illusion a little more to our benefit, and our frustration that the world we perceive isn't a flawless rendition of what we imagine would be perfection.

It's a human tendency to try to make life (Samsara) comfortable. We (especially a lot of Westerners) have very high expectations for that. We want a nice house (but it always needs improving), a nice car (but maybe a newer model), a nice body (which could *really* use improving!), and on and on. As we go through the day, the people we encounter could use improving. We need a new, more appreciative boss. We need more friends, or the ones we have could treat us better. We need a lover, or the one we already have could use a makeover—or maybe we want a newer model there too. Though this is a universal human tendency, I think it's become particularly prevalent in modern life among those of us with enough options to feel dissatisfied. Even if we don't have so many options, we're bombarded by media that shows us all the wonderful options we should probably want.

Until a century ago, humans hardly threw anything away and were more likely to stay within the communities, and in the relationships, they already had—often because they had no other choices, and because they weren't inundated with images, products, media, and an economy that encouraged dissatisfaction with the status quo. Now, to be content with what—and who—one has seems almost unpatriotic. Nearly every TV ad (for new cars, medications, food and drink, dating sites, and bigger and brighter TVs on which to watch these same ads) relies on the assumption that what we have isn't as good as what we could get next. As one lama, Gyatrul Rinpoche, told a friend, "Americans are masters at selling Samsara."

I've often found myself stuck in the swirling eddy of "if-onlys," as I call them. If only my sweetheart didn't do this. If only my boss didn't do that. If only, if only, if only . . . THEN I would be happy. From this expectation of life, we generate endless if-onlys, which give birth to baby if-onlys, and then those babies have babies, all of which multiply and grow. What a powerless position to be in. Not a very happy mental loop to spend my time in, I know. Yet when I was younger, I think I spent a majority of my time in some form of the if-onlys. Now I still spend time there, but a whole lot less, and it's easier for me to notice and move out of it. It's taken a lot of practice for me to get this far. Luckily the practice usually feels good.

Good thing Rinpoche didn't wait for the if-onlys to come true while he was in prison.

Remember the renowned physicist, David Bohm, and his Holo-movement? I talked about it in Book 1, along with his ideas about the "implicate" and "explicate" order. He saw the universe as a hologram, and it was constantly flashing back and forth between the "implicate order" and the "explicate order"—a bit like the frames of a movie, with the dark parts in between. We see a continuity in the explicate parts—the parts with images. But that's not how Bohm saw it . . . nor did the Buddha. They both used the ocean metaphor. And if we see that we're not just wave but also ocean, we don't have the pressure of needing those if-onlys.

And what about the "order" part of Bohm's idea? He believed that, since the universe is a hologram, with the whole thing within each part and vice versa, then to see any part as separate and independent is wrong. And a wrong view of reality always leads to a painful collision with how reality really is. Just remember back to when you liked somebody, and thought they liked you back, and you discovered they didn't. Ouch!

Late in his life, Bohm did an interview with Renée Weber* in which he sounded very Buddhist, despite being a Jewish physicist. At one point he described the structure of the universe in this way:

BOHM   *The present state of theoretical physics implies that empty space has all this energy and [that] matter is a slight increase of the energy, having some relative stability, and being manifest. Now, therefore, my suggestion is that this implicate order implies a reality immensely beyond what we call matter. Matter itself is merely a ripple in this background.*

WEBER   In this ocean of energy, you are saying.

BOHM   *In this ocean of energy. And the ocean of energy is not primarily in space and time at all: it's primarily in the implicate order.*

WEBER   Which is to say unmanifest, not manifest.

BOHM   *Right. And it may manifest in this little bit of matter.*

WEBER   The ripple.

BOHM   *The ripple, you see.*

---

*   "The Enfolding-Unfolding Universe: A Conversation with David Bohm"; © 1978 by David Bohm. This appears as Chapter 5 in the book edited by Ken Wilber: *The Holographic Paradigm and Other Paradoxes* (Boston: New Science Library 1982) pp. 44–104.

Mind . . . blown. Bohm then goes on to apply that same hologram idea to humanity and its present, confused state. Just as we can't see the universe as he and physicists are discovering it to be, likewise we don't see ourselves in true relationship to humanity. Both of these misperceptions, together, are the root of our present problems. Bohm says that we can find our way out of this mess we've stumbled into, and it can start with one person cleaning up their act when it comes to perceiving reality.

As you or I might wonder, Weber asked him if one person could really change the consciousness of all of humanity. Bohm said that it was "damp" because of the eons of misperception, so it would take the "passion", the "energy" of a few people seeing the same thing—true relationship of individual and whole—together. "And if ten people can have their part of consciousness all one, that is an energy which begins to spread into the whole."

I've explained that Samsara, this movie we've made with us as the star, is flawed from the beginning. It's a setup for suffering. I suggest that we lower our expectations of Samsara. (There's a bumper sticker for you: *Let's lower our expectations of Samsara.*) Rather than looking to Samsara to make you happy—a losing proposition—look to, and for, the path out of it. If we're having a bad dream, the sensible thing seems to be to wake up. Oddly enough, an early step along that path seems to be *accepting* what/who/where is happening. Not to succumb to it, necessarily, but to accept that it *is* happening. A big first step in Alcoholics Anonymous, as well as successful diet programs, is that new-comers accept the state they're in, the situation that brought them to seek a way out.

Let's lower our expectations of Samsara.

The more you train your mind not to follow after every thought spawned by desire and aggression, hope and fear, the freer you are. Chasing your hopes and illusions, your fears and your aversions, in your mind or your life isn't real freedom. It isn't real happiness either. But how can you free yourself from want and not-want if you're expecting happiness in this fatally flawed existence? We want what we think is in our grasp. In Samsara, true happiness is always out of reach.

The reason I'm going into all this is to get down to what many lamas have told us in various ways: the first step on the path out of Samsara is to get good and fed up with it.

The reason I'm going into all this is to get down to what many lamas have told us in various ways: the first step on the path out of Samsara is to get good and fed up with it.

Yet if we're identified with the whole ocean, there's nothing that we need, and no wave is a threat to us. If we're living from the point of view of the ocean rather than protecting or indulging all the desires of this one "me" wave, we can afford to love everyone fully.

If you love and accept everyone *except* so-and-so (if only they'd *behave* better—and by "better," I mean "the way I want them to"), then how will you be able to open your heart and really practice *Boundless Loving Kindness*? Your own heart will always remain a bit smaller—a bit shriveled. His Holiness the Dalai Lama has plenty of reason to resent the Chinese, but he refuses to let any grievances or provocation tempt him to shrivel his heart. And it's his undiminished heart that earned him the Nobel Peace Prize,

> "My religion is very simple. My religion is kindness."
>
> *His Holiness the Dalai Lama XIV*

and has made him one of the most beloved people on the planet. Rather than causing him any pain, his indiscriminate loving of people keeps him smiling (thus the original title of this series, *Why Is the Dalai Lama Always Smiling?*).

We can pursue that Boundless love in our own lives, in our own ways. Why not?

Do we have something better to do?

BOUNDLESS
(IMMEASURABLE) EQUANIMITY

You might wonder why I'm starting with the last Boundless Quality. As I've said, without this one, the others won't be Boundless, so we need to cultivate this one first—and in practicing the others—so that as we practice them over time, we'll feel increasingly connected to all and everyone. This is the correcting of the habit of mind that David Bohm was referring to. It has its own direct reward as well. As the Zen saying goes, "Enlightenment is easy . . . for those who have no preferences." How do we cultivate this open-minded, open-hearted perspective?

In this particular application of equanimity, we aren't referring to preference of one flavor of ice cream over another. While in Buddhist thought, equanimity in that more general sense is seen as a key capacity, here we're focusing on one particular application of it. In Boundless Equanimity, we're specifically referring to feeling as strongly and lovingly connected to all beings as we are to our favorite ones.

> In Boundless Equanimity, we're specifically referring
> to feeling as strongly and lovingly connected to
> all beings as we are to our favorite ones.

If you accept the phenomenon of reincarnation, then you can imagine that, in the countless lifetimes since beginningless time, you, and the others around you right now, have played every imaginable role with each other. Today's friend was our enemy in some other life. Our child was our murderer. And before that, we murdered them. If you do the math, you could figure that, in an infinite number of lives, every single being in all of Samsara was our parent, caring for us like those baby birds (which is why, as I've mentioned before, Buddhists often refer to other beings as our "mothers.")

And because everyone has been our parent at some point, everyone we know now has been that caring to us in some lifetime–maybe more than one. And of course we care a LOT about those who have nurtured us—we care whether they live or die, are suffering or happy, or are in turmoil or at peace. So even though some of you may not feel that way about your (current) parents—it might be love mixed with resentment, annoyance, and other conflicting feelings—there's surely somebody you *do* feel that way about. Who might that be? In a class I was teaching, one woman said she couldn't think of anyone she felt such affection for. I don't know why but I said, "Do you have a cat?" She did! Of course she melted as she thought of her cat. After billions of lifetimes, odds are you've felt that way about every being, human or otherwise.

Many of you may not be so sure about reincarnation. (Understood. I'm sure that in some of my previous lives I was skeptical about reincarnation, too!) But you don't have to factor in reincarnation in order to cultivate Boundless Equanimity. Just look at this lifetime.

Strangers have become friends; friends have become estranged; allies have become enemies and vice versa. We care deeply for friends and family, but they can also be a distraction that keeps us from practice, not to mention other beneficial opportunities. Or they can turn on us, inflicting our greatest pain and suffering. On the other hand, our enemies can be the most help to us. The Buddha was thankful toward Devadatta, his lifetime nemesis, because the challenge of working with Devadatta's attacks spurred the Buddha on in his practice.

If we think in this broader way, hopefully it helps us to expand the usual bounds we have around who we care about and how much we care.

My friends from other countries have noticed that the news in the US is very American-centric. In an international disaster we often only hear about the number of Americans killed. I assume this is because American media know that Americans care much more about fellow Americans. And the more the news reports in this American-centric way, the more Americans become American-centric. Eventually we might even want to make it official and build a wall. Whoops, we did.

Fall at the Namchak Retreat Ranch

Looking south across the hills on the west side of the valley of Namchak Retreat Ranch

This idea of "my" country, "my" people is a natural consequence to the idea of "I," or ego. Yes, there's that old troublemaker again. If we only care (feel connected with) "my people," then our hearts are already smaller and, well, more disconnected. This isn't going to help our poverty of heart. These Four Boundless Qualities practices gradually erode that habit and replace it with something both real and deeply satisfying.

What about the checkout lady at the grocery store? She means nothing to you now. If you accept reincarnation, then in some lifetime she was probably your parent or your child. Even in this lifetime she could possibly marry your brother or sister. And in this lifetime, for sure, she feels just as much suffering as you do when bad things happen to her, and just as much happiness at the good things. She's a sentient being, just like you and me.

If you work in concentric circles, you can train in Equanimity, eventually making it truly Boundless by including all your fellow sentient beings in your circle of caring, loving connection. I think you'll find that in spending that caring, love, and compassion on the checkout lady, you haven't lost a thing. You'll actually feel a deep, rich sense of expanded love/expanded heart.

DOING THE PRACTICE OF BOUNDLESS EQUANIMITY

I'm giving you a more involved description here, but for your everyday sessions, you can use the practice card for this, folded (the practice, not the card!) into the Round Robin practice, in the back pocket of the book. Those practice cards, as with the last book, are meant to live on your practice table and go with you when you travel. I've also included a card of this practice folded into the Round Robin practice at the end of this section too.

Because we want to feel as strongly connected to all beings as to our favorite pet, we want to prime the pump by feeling those warm feelings that come easily for our pet, our child, our lover. Then we can expand that out, rung by rung of concentric circles, to feel those same feelings just as strongly for all beings. You might not feel those feelings so strongly for yourself, but you're a sentient being too. And if you don't love yourself, what basis will you have for loving anybody else really well?

Some people find that because they don't love themselves very much, or were programmed that it's prideful to love and care for yourself in any way, they respond better when they start with another for whom they can easily rouse those warm, caring feelings. Find which hits the spot for you. Once you're feeling strongly and positively toward your favorite person or critter, you can keep those feelings going, and bring them in to yourself. And then another deep breath, relaxing into it. It might take a few tries, but that's why they call it practice!

What could be more true and natural than the love from the source of us all, coming through to one of its creations—a wave on and of the ocean? I seriously believe that if everyone did this practice there would be more peace between people.

Once you're feeling that warm connection—getting past our usual distraction from the way things truly are—you then allow those feelings to roll out to more people. So the next rung out is still people and critters you easily feel warmth and affection for: you give them each a hug, or just smile warmly back and forth.

Continue to the next rung—the guy at the checkout counter at the grocery store, or someone at work whom you hardly know. Both, why not?! The tide of warm, affectionate caring continues rolling out to all of the people in the category you'd normally call "indifferent" until you actually feel anything but. They are now beloveds, fellow waves on the ocean, wanting happiness and not wanting suffering, just like you. You can feel the truth of your connection.

Now the tide of warm connection rolls out to include all beings. Pick a few particular kinds to make it more real. All people in whatever building you're in; all people in your town; all the mice, squirrels, birds, and other animals who live near you; everyone (as in all sentient beings) in the county; the state; your whole country; your whole hemisphere; Earth; other worlds.

Rest for a moment, in this delicious, warm feeling. Write something down in your journal about how you feel, in that particular session, that particular moment.

Dedicate the merit. The positive karma you generated, from that work on yourself and the good thoughts you put into the atmosphere, to all beings reaching ultimate happiness, forever.

By now you're no doubt ready to spend around fifteen to twenty-five minutes per session. Please *give* yourself that *gift*. It will benefit you and many others, if you do. Besides, *it feels good!*

Sample Daily Practice Session #1
ROUND ROBIN MEDITATION WITH THE
FOUR BOUNDLESS QUALITIES

- **1 MINUTE OR LESS:** Check motivation for doing this practice, in *this* session. Bring forward Bodhisattva motivation (the Two Purposes) if necessary. (Remember: it almost always needs a little bringing forward, but don't expect it to be one hundred percent before going ahead to the practice—that's what the practice is *for*, after all.)

- **60 TO 90 SECONDS:** Clearing the Stale Energies Rest.

- **21 BREATHS OF SHAMATA FOLLOWED BY A FEW MINUTES OF SHAMATA**

- **10 TO 15 MINUTES:** Equanimity, Loving Kindness, Tonglen (Compassion), or Sympathetic Joy (One at a time. Again, if it feels like time to switch from Compassion to Joy, for example, go for it.)

- **10 TO 15 MINUTES:** Shamata
  (*Optional:* If you have the time, you could alternate between Shamata and one of the Four Boundless Qualities again and again. Generally, you would finish with at least a little bit of Shamata before moving on to the concluding prayers.)

- **30 SECONDS:** Dedication of merit

DEDICATION AND ASPIRATION

> *By the power of this compassionate practice*
> *May suffering be transformed into peace.*
> *May the hearts of all beings be open,*
> *And their wisdom radiate from within.*

(Courtesy of the *Tergar Sangha*)

BOUNDLESS (IMMEASURABLE) LOVING KINDNESS

Continuing our "Bodhicitta Workout," expanding our capacity of heart, we've now come to the training on Loving Kindness. Remember, we're working with strong feelings of love, which we then step out in concentric circles, just as we do with Boundless Equanimity and with Compassion in Tonglen. As with the others, I strongly recommend starting with yourself, or if that's not so easy for you, someone for whom Loving Kindness comes easily.

His Holiness the Dalai Lama was absolutely amazed when longtime Western Dharma students told him that most Westerners weren't so sure they loved themselves. He thought all of us humans loved ourselves the best. Not so. In many cases, we Westerners are rather ambivalent, having an unstable, conditional, love/hate relationship with ourselves. In fact, many of us dislike ourselves. True, we're fascinated with and fixated on ourselves, but affectionate Loving Kindness for ourselves can be sorely missing. At first His Holiness didn't believe this. Perhaps many Tibetan lamas still don't. But he was finally convinced.

My lama, Tulku Sangak Rinpoche, always looks confused when Westerners report this to him.

Another Tibetan lama, Mingyur Rinpoche, also couldn't imagine what his Western students were talking about on this subject. He was determined to find out, because he felt that without truly understanding this *in his bones,* he wouldn't be able to help those students connect with the Dharma. So he decided to cultivate a bad opinion of himself. First he grilled some of his top Western students, to find out exactly where the negative opinions came from, and how they worked.

Then every day, in meditation and in between, he focused on his faults and shortcomings. He told himself that because of these, he was intrinsically worthless. He gave himself all kinds of similar negative messages. One day he realized that he was feeling little love for himself. He felt rather depressed. Then he thought, "YAY! Now I get it! Now I don't like myself either—*how wonderful!*" Now, that's compassion. Needless to say, he resumed his usual practices and came back to his usual joyful state.

So: start with love and affection for yourself.

Boundless Loving Kindness—The Practice

You can kindle positive feelings for yourself in a variety of ways. How you do that could vary. Be imaginative, change it up once in a while, to keep it alive and fresh. You might either imagine yourself in front of or inside your heart, as you did with Tonglen. It's your practice session; you get to do what you like. Nobody's going to report you. Whatever works—especially since, as a Westerner, starting with Loving Kindness for yourself is already a new notion.

You envelop yourself in warm, strong feelings of love. Perhaps it comes in waves. Perhaps you have waves of tears, like a person in the desert coming to water at last. Perhaps you can't even take too much of it at once. You might have to build your capacity gradually.

(I was tempted to joke that narcissists could skip this part, but narcissism isn't actually Boundless, unconditional Loving Kindness toward oneself—because it lacks the essential element of equanimity. A narcissist doesn't feel that they, like all of creation, are unconditionally lovable; a narcissist believes that they're better than everyone else, uniquely deserving of praise, attention, and high regard.)

Maybe you have a protective crust around your heart that you unconsciously put there long ago. People try to insulate themselves from the pain of missing out on love or, worse yet, the pain of rejection. But this perspective and practice provides a safe, dependable source of love and warmth. So slowly, slowly, we can reverse that habit.

As we've noted, another unconscious assumption that keeps us from loving ourselves is the message we somehow got that we're not *worthy* of love. We think that we have to be perfect to be lovable—and we know we're not perfect.

In fact, most of us believe we're *essentially* flawed. But once we begin to experience how we come from that one great ocean/source that's

> None of the people we love are even close to perfect—and we love them anyway. Why set an impossibly higher standard for ourselves?

perfect—*this* wave that's made of nothing but the ocean's water—we come to our own true essence, which Buddhists call Buddha Nature. No matter how much confusion is covering that over, our true nature can never be sullied. Like water with dirt in it, once we filter out the dirt, that water is still water. Even *with* the dirt, it's still water. We can base our love on that. Then we can recognize it in others and base that Boundless Loving Kindness on that. (In the interim, we can also remind ourselves that none of the people we love are even close to perfect—and we love them anyway. Why set an impossibly higher standard for ourselves?)

Think of your own nature as a sentient being, a fleck of that ocean of awareness, your essence pure from the beginningless origins of time. Of course you want to be happy. Of course you don't want to suffer. You now envelop yourself with the wish for this one—you—to be supremely happy always, and never to suffer even a little. Be like

that mother bird with her babies. Don't you think her babies deserve
it? Then why not you? What's the difference?

As we noted earlier, "Love thy neighbor as thyself" only works if you
love thyself. That's the basis for the rest of it. Otherwise, your neighbor's not getting much of a deal: "Love thy neighbor as you loathe
yourself" doesn't have quite the same ring.

> "Love thy neighbor as thyself" only works if you love
> thyself. That's the basis for the rest of it. Otherwise, your
> neighbor's not getting much of a deal: "Love thy neighbor
> as you loathe yourself" doesn't have quite the same ring.

I imagine myself actually embracing myself; giving myself a long,
warm hug. At the same time I feel myself getting the hug, really relaxing into it and taking it in. The Theravadins, who do this practice a
lot, call it Metta. They say this for every sentient being (you, included):

May you be happy. May you be well. May you be safe. May you be
peaceful and at ease.

Once you have a reasonably strong feeling of love for yourself in
this *healthy* way (again, we're not talking about ego clinging, inflation,
or self-absorption) you begin to step it out. Begin with another you
already easily feel this love for. See them clearly before you. Hold them
in the warm embrace of love. Then you might say the sentences above,
to them. Keep going till you feel strong feelings of love, like waves
rolling out to that person. (HINT: This will work much better if you did
true Loving Kindness for yourself and really took it in. And again, we
don't mean self-centered narcissism but just the love that is natural to
that great ocean/source of all.)

Continue with a few more individuals. The tide is getting stronger
now. You could even pick that store checkout guy or lady, and others you don't know well. Now, with the tide rolling out so strongly,
you think, "Sure, I want this woman to be totally, ecstatically happy!
Wouldn't that be great?!" You still don't even know the woman's name,
but you're really rooting for her everlasting joy. Why not? This is feeling really good.

Then, as with Tonglen, you work with whole classes of beings. Pre-
school students, hospital patients, that lady at the checkout counter,

beautiful dancers you saw on TV—*all* dancers: ballet dancers, hula dancers, exotic dancers, fire dancers, pole dancers—why not? All stray dogs, *all* dogs, all the different kinds of wild animals. Then there are the seas full of sentient beings. And bugs—bugs have feelings too. How's that for a bumper sticker? All mothers, all fathers, all who were ever mothers or fathers . . . which would be every sentient being.

Not only are many of us American-centered, but we all tend to be rather Earth-centered—understandably! But according to modern science, there are *so* many stars in the universe and so many planets, that it's highly unlikely we would be the only planet supporting life forms. The Buddha taught much the same thing, and that there are other planes of existence that we can't perceive. So we do our best to expand our Loving Kindness to ALL sentient beings. Who knows, maybe last life we were on one of those planes or planets ourselves!

Stick with that much for your Round Robin sessions for a couple of weeks. That's a lot! Once you're ready, you can add in a rung for people who annoy you, just before the "all beings" rung at the end. Those annoying people are sentient beings too. They're trying to pursue happiness and avoid suffering, using the best methods they know of. We could say just the same for you and me. To slightly paraphrase the Buddha, hate never eradicates hate. Only love can do that.

In a few weeks you might work up to troublemakers in your life. Eventually you could try including people who have caused you significant harm. Please don't get too ambitious with this one. Approach it with caution. You might or might not be ready to do this one on the day you think you should. In many cases, I'd recommend reading the section on forgiveness in this book, and possibly working with a good therapist. Again, psychotherapy can come at it from one direction, and your practice can from another.

We spend a fair amount of time trying to figure out how we can get that pain-in-the-butt person out of our lives, and we usually can't. Even if we manage some big power play and push them out, we often end up like Hercules and the hydra: every time he cut off one head, two would appear in its place. Nowadays we can look at the US method of handling the Middle East and it feels about the same.

Here's a very different method, which His Holiness the Dalai Lama recommends: transform an enemy into a friend. Not everyone will be receptive, but if we begin by transforming our own feelings toward that person, we have a chance of stopping our war with them. For sure we can stop it inside our own hearts. That already feels better. The Indian saint, Neem Karoli Baba, said, "Never throw anyone out of your heart." It makes your own heart smaller. How can Loving Kindness be Boundless if we do that?

Now you've hopefully included every being in all of existence. How do you feel, compared with when you started? Try keeping a journal by your meditation spot. I do. For one thing, questions come up, and I know I'll forget one or another, just when I get the chance to ask one of my teachers. If I jot down a note or two about my practice experience after a session, I find it makes it more *real*, in my mind. Otherwise, it sort of evaporates and it's like it never happened. It also will help crystalize your thoughts and feelings now, and someday in the future you can look back and appreciate all that has happened on

Does that annoying person at work look like this?

your journey. Because we want to extract as much learning as possible, occasional reflection on our experience—rather than constantly charging headlong—makes all the difference.

You don't need to stop when you get up from meditation. Why wouldn't you want to continue this feeling throughout the day, with everyone you meet? As the beloved master Shantideva says in his classic *The Way of the Bodhisattva,* "Whenever catching sight of others, look on them with open, loving heart." I know this is something we all want to do, and not just because we're supposed to. It *feels better.* Techniques such as this one help more fully, with ever more people. I'm not telling you this because it sounds good. It's from my own personal experience.

WHAT ABOUT THOSE
WHO HAVE HURT ME?

Let us be practical and ask the question, "How do we love our enemies?"
First, we must develop and maintain the capacity to forgive. He who
is devoid of the power to forgive is devoid of the power to love.

—DR. MARTIN LUTHER KING, JR. in *Strength to Love*

I'm not going to lie, it's really hard sometimes to feel love for
someone who has hurt and/or wronged us. That is why I find Dr.
King's question so important: *how* do we love our enemies? Maybe
you wouldn't call them an enemy; maybe it's just a difficult person, a
beloved who has wronged you, or a garden-variety troublemaker. *How*
do we get from resenting them to loving them? But even before that,

Far away view of the Mission Mountain Range from the Three-Year Retreat

we often have to ask the question, *why* should I? I'm right and they're wrong. I'm the injured party. They should apologize and make it right but they won't. Or they do, and you still don't feel satisfied. After all, "I'm sorry" doesn't undo all damage.

First let me say what forgiveness *isn't*. It's not having selective amnesia. You don't have to forget what happened, in order to forgive. What a relief! Second, you don't have to condone or even slightly agree with what they did. Absolutely not necessary. Remember, there's a huge difference between what someone *did* and who they *are*—their true essence.

Pure essence aside for a moment, let's be honest: Everybody is quite capable of *behaving* well and *behaving* badly. Both. Even you and I. Mahatma Gandhi slept with women other than his wife, and Hitler was kind to his niece. It helps me to remember those facts—

both that the person who hurt me is capable of behaving well (and their essential nature is pure) *and* I'm capable of behaving badly or being mistaken. I sometimes wonder how I would feel or behave if I were treated badly for years on end, in a US prison, for example—or in a concentration camp. As the years wore on, would I get more resentful, desperate, and crazy? Under the pressure of a crazy system, would I finally commit acts I would never previously have guessed that I would? I honestly don't know.

If Dr. King was going to wait for all the prejudiced people to apologize and make it right for him and other Black people, he'd have waited all of his life and then some. Meanwhile he'd be weighing down his own heart with resentment. He would be adding to his suffering, and it wouldn't help anyone. It wouldn't hurt his oppressors. Because he found a way to lighten his heart of that heavy load, not only was he happier, the world is a better place because of the hard work he did inside.

Remember the part of Tulku Sangak Rinpoche's story, in Book 1, when he was in prison and suffering more from his own resentment than from the actions of the guards? With the guidance of lamas and the benefits of his practice, he was able to turn his experience completely around. He actually enjoyed prison! But the first step was for him to *decide to offload his resentment.*

Rinpoche didn't begin by practicing Loving Kindness, Compassion, and Forgiveness for the guards for their sake. He began by doing it for his own sake. Later he came to practice it for their sake, which might or might not have improved things for them. But it certainly did for him.

I love that quote attributed to Neem Karoli Baba, "Never throw anyone out of your heart." That includes people who have wronged you. As I thought about that little quote, which is actually a real challenge, I slowly came to appreciate how powerful it was. It challenged me to look into my own heart and see that where I held onto even a small bit of resentment, my heart shrank a bit. It was a bit darker and heavier.

With each grudge that I let go of, or even lessened, my heart became more capable of love, and more joyful. The world just a bit more beautiful; the colors more vivid.

Looking at that, I realized it was an ongoing feeling, way, way in the background. I came to understand the accuracy of the phrase, "nursing a grudge." I didn't want to feed any of them anymore. When I've unearthed a slowly smoldering grudge, much to my horror it turned out to be a forest fire waiting to happen. Luckily I had practices I could apply, to work it through and actually resolve it. My heart immediately felt settled, lighter, and fuller, all together. With each grudge that I let go of, or even lessened, my heart became more capable of love, and more joyful. The world just a bit more beautiful; the colors more vivid.

And that's just the effect on *me.* Can you imagine the effect on anyone in contact with me? As I've said before, thoughts and views are contagious. If someone cuts you off in traffic while giving you the One-Finger Salute, do you feel all warm and fuzzy? On the other hand (without one finger extended), a woman told me of a young couple that was deeply in love, basking in each other's presence while waiting for their airplane. Everyone at the gate was sneaking peeks at them, their faces lit up with warm smiles.

Let's extend that out a bit. Now those people might just treat each other a little better as they're feeling love themselves. Those people then are just a little more kind and loving, and touch yet more people. Imagine if everyone did the practice—yes, it can be a conscious practice—of forgiveness and freed up their hearts, felt more connected to everyone?

And what about the opposite? Tribes are trying to wipe each other out, in retribution for what the other tribes did to them. Some of these feuds have been going on for hundreds, if not thousands of years. Not so long ago, there was an eruption of the age-old feuding in the former Balkan states.

Again in his book, *Strength to Love,* Dr. King had this to say:

> *Upheaval after upheaval has reminded us that modern man is traveling along a road called hate, in a journey that will bring us to destruction and damnation. Far from being the pious injunction of a Utopian dreamer, the command to love one's enemy is an absolute necessity for our survival. Love even for enemies is the key to the solution of the problems of our world. Jesus is not an impractical idealist: he is the practical realist.*

Although Dr. King wrote that sometime before he died in 1968, that paragraph is even more timely today.

When I was in my twenties, my father thought I was charmingly naive about the world. He was a kindhearted man, and at the same time, saw himself as a pragmatist. As you may remember from Book 1, he was also a consummate debater. Hoping to lure me into a position he could then undercut, he said, "You think if everyone just loved each other, we'd solve all the world's problems." I thought of the brilliance of the human mind, that figured out how to put a person on the moon not too long before. I thought that if we loved each other we would apply ourselves to solving problems like feeding everyone while preserving the environment. War would be unthinkable. My mind flashed through thoughts such as this. I looked him in the eye and simply replied, "Yes, I do." We looked at each other for a long moment of silence. The debate was over before it had begun.

SCIENCE TIDBIT

Forgiveness

Whether it's for a huge disagreement or actions we'd all agree are terrible, resentment certainly has some very bad effects on us. The article "Forgiveness: Your Health Depends On It" quotes Karen Swartz, M.D., director of the Adult Mood Disorders Consultation Clinic at The Johns Hopkins Hospital. Swartz says, "There is an enormous physical burden to being hurt and disappointed." The article then says, "Chronic anger puts you into a fight-or-flight mode, which results in numerous changes in heart rate, blood pressure, and immune response."* None of them are good. Though studies on the effects of resentment versus forgiveness used to be quite rare, in the last decade or so they have become much more common. All of the ones I've seen show the same ill effects of grudges as the article mentioned above.

Not surprisingly, in numerous studies forgiveness has been shown to have the opposite effects of resentment. Heart rate, blood pressure, and immune response all improve with forgiveness. In some studies, even on the same person, the resentment produced negative readings in all of the above categories. Then a bit later, as the same subjects changed to feelings of empathy or were practicing forgiveness, the biometrics shifted to positive readings in all the same physiological categories.**

STUDENT *I'm sold on the idea that resentment isn't good for me and that I'd be better off forgiving.*

That makes sense. But come on, my father physically abused me regularly throughout my childhood. Am I supposed to just ignore that—pretend it never happened? But there are very real, lasting effects on me, and no doubt my children, as a result.

LT First, I just want to say how very sad I am, to hear that you grew up in that environment, where someone who was supposed to care for you and keep you safe actually harmed

---

* Johns Hopkins Medicine. "Forgiveness: Your Health Depends on It." Retrieved from https://www.hopkinsmedicine.org/health/wellness-and-prevention/forgiveness-your-health-depends-on-it on Feb. 21, 2022.

** Van Oyen Witvliet, Charlotte, Thomas E. Ludwig, and Kelly L. Vander Laan, "Granting Forgiveness or Harboring Grudges: Implications for Emotions, Physiology, and Health." *Psychological Science*, no. 12 (2001): 117–23. https://doi.org/10.1111/1467-9280.00320

BACK TO YOU ON THE CUSHION

That's all very well, but how do we get from here to there? Forget managing to get the whole world to love each other, how do I get myself to love everybody when I still have gripes with my parents or my power-crazed boss? I genuinely believe that we start changing the world by changing our own hearts. Practicing the Four Boundless Qualities regularly has changed the hearts of many people, including thousands of people in various scientific studies. I have used these Qualities to change my own. I see it as a great place to start on the world.

you instead. I'm quite sure you did and do experience the effects from that, even today. The hard truth is that you can't go back and change what happened. That said, when memory is tested scientifically, it turns out that it's much more elastic than we used to think it was. This has caused endless problems with witnesses in police stations and courts of law. Dr. Peter Levine has done some groundbreaking work, actually *using* our elastic memories, in healing trauma. Intrigued? I was fascinated. He talks about it in his groundbreaking book, *Waking the Tiger*.

But that doesn't change the fact that this did happen to you, and luckily you don't have to have amnesia or creative memory in order to drop that heavy grudge. In testing people who had been deeply wronged by another, some were holding on to the resentment and some had forgiven their transgressor. You might not be surprised to know that when the grudge-holders thought of the person they resented, their blood pressure, heart rate, cortisol (a fight-or-flight chemical), and other readings went into the "danger zone" while their immune systems were suppressed, showing worse effects than any other kind of stress. Of course they also showed painful emotions like anger, frustration, and so on. The opposite was true of the ones who forgave.

These studies give credence to the old saying, "Hating someone is like drinking poison and expecting the other person to die."

Dr. King was aware that indulging Righteous Wrath can be a huge obstacle to stepping these Four Boundless Qualities out to include all beings.

But if we exclude from our hearts George, who was my friend who turned on me, or Mom, who mostly ignored me (not my own mom, by the way), we aren't including all beings. If we try to practice this finishing up with, "All beings except George . . . " how does that feel? As I said above, when I do it I can feel my heart remaining a bit shrunken and closed. Also I can't help but focus on George sometimes. If I try to do the practices without thinking of George (or whomever I feel hurt by) but I'm still secretly loading my heart down with resentment about George, I'm depriving myself of the benefit of the practice. Meanwhile, need I mention that my resentment isn't causing any problems for George? Only for me.

So far I've only mentioned grudges over actions that almost all of us would agree are wrong. But there are also sometimes actions that two people might not agree are wrong. I have no idea how many grudges are carried over simple disagreements, but I imagine quite a few. Another popular source of grudges is our discomfort when a person touches on one of our sore spots. Rather than looking to see if it might be our own sore spot that's the main source of our pain, we look outwardly and blame it on the person who happened to touch on it. Whatever the original cause of hurt, grudges can lead to actions that are just plain wrong in anyone's eyes.

STUDENT   *I guess that makes sense. But if I forgive him, aren't I saying it's okay? But it's never okay for a parent to beat their child. The objective truth is that I'm right.*

LT   Yes, you're right. There are very few people in the world who would think your dad's actions were right, or good for you. Now what?

Now what?

Look, I know that because you're right, it's *really tempting* to hold on to the grudge. I see myself indulging in it sometimes. I call it the Righteous Wrath Reason. But once you've acknowledged you're right, what good *to you* is that righteous wrath? What harm is it doing them? Bottom line, if it's not doing you any good, why indulge it? I'd love to see a bumper sticker out there that says, "If righteous wrath isn't doing you any good, why indulge it?" Let me put this another way, because it's so important: You don't forgive for the benefit of the person who harmed you. *You do it for you.* And for all of us.

I do believe this righteous wrath is an indulgence, and as we've seen above, it's an expensive one. Maybe that's another bumper sticker: "Righteous wrath is an expensive indulgence." Seriously, I think it might be at least as expensive as indulging in smoking cigarettes. And perhaps equally addictive.

As with many addictions, it can ruin your life. My dad told me of a friend of his who had been terribly wronged in his business. The other guy got away with it, and my dad's friend—we'll call him Julius—was left with a financial mess and a family to support. He was furious! And he was right. The other guy had embezzled, broken the law, and was unquestionably in the wrong. Now what? Julius couldn't get over it. The more he thought about it, the angrier he got. The angrier he got, the more he thought about it. Everything reminded him of that betrayal.

> Righteous wrath is an expensive indulgence.

Julius ended up in the hospital. His colon had gotten tied in a knot. The doctors would need to do a serious operation to cut and unknot his gut. My dad was not even slightly into holistic health or mind/body workshops in California, but he was pretty sure how this medical condition came about.

He visited Julius in the hospital and said, "Your resentment is literally tying your guts in knots. For God's sake, Julius, you've got to let go of this."

The downward spiral of resentment is something any of us could fall into. Dr. Fred Luskin outlines the few simple steps by which we take ourselves there. As with addiction, a huge factor is habit. Alcoholics Anonymous members say that it's the countless, habitual little steps leading up to taking the drink that are the place to do the work. It's those steps that lead to the "inevitable" and irresistible step of taking that drink. In the case of negative mind loops such as resentment, I think it's like Netflix. Really! Both on Netflix and in our minds, there are thousands of movies available anytime. We just have to click on one. Our brains are capable of focusing conscious awareness on only one at a time.

You could focus on the movie about your father who abused you, or you could focus on the wonderful dog you had when you were growing up. Maybe you have a wonderful dog right now. Again, your conscious mind can only focus on one thing at a time. Which will it be—your father's abuse or the dog? Or your father's taking you on an adventure? Which movie are you going to go to? Some people watch horror and disaster movies all the time; others tend to watch romantic comedies. There are tons of different movies in your mind. You're a grown-up now. You can decide which movie to watch.

But even though you're outwardly free to decide, there's the undertow of habit. The more you indulge resentful or vengeful thoughts about George who wronged you, the more your brain will fall into playing and watching that movie. That cycle builds momentum that's easier and easier to get swept away by. The undertow. In retreat, I've found my mind in this or that loop, playing the same movie again and

again. I'm completely bored with that movie, but here it is, coming around again. As with any habit, it takes commitment and, at first, a lot of watchfulness to catch yourself and reroute your mind to the movie you constantly choose. Gradually, as you continue to do it, your mind more and more easily plays the movies on your new list. After some time, you can find that your mind goes to those movies as habitually as it used to dwell on the resentful ones.

I hasten to add that as a psychotherapist (and person who's been wronged and had to forgive), I believe that with bigger wrongs that you've suffered, a good psychotherapist can be helpful too. But I've seen people stuck in psychotherapy for years, blaming their parent or sibling from their childhood for their present issues, and nothing getting resolved. I believe the two approaches together can bring us the most freedom.

I don't happen to know of studies about resenting jobs (though they probably exist), but I sure hear people talking about it. Frida hated and resented hers, and went to a wise woman for advice on how to be rid of it. The wise woman said, "You're spending so much time thinking about all the ways you hate your job, that your mind is actually keeping you there. Find ways to like your job and you'll be able to be free of it."

"Oh great," Frida thought. "All I have to do to leave my sucky job is to think it's wonderful." The next day she glumly went to work and looked around for *something* redeeming about the place. Her eyes landed on a picture on the wall, of a quiet forest scene. She certainly liked it—she'd picked it out herself! She brought her mind back to that beautiful picture again and again. Then she thought of a co-worker she was friends with. She did always enjoy seeing her there. She focused on the co-worker. Slowly but surely—much to her amazement—she stepped from one thing to the next until she really didn't mind going to work. In fact, after a few weeks she noticed something she would never have thought possible: she now looked forward to going to work. No one was more surprised than Frida! Naturally, shortly after that, a side project she had been working on blossomed and she could make a living doing that. She was able to quit her job!

Again, once we've been in the habit of beating a path to the disaster and righteous wrath movies, it takes some self-awareness to stop and find our way to inspirational movies. One simple, tangible little practice we can do is to keep a Gratitude Attitude journal. I've kept one for a long time, as have many students, and it has really helped us all to reroute ourselves to the more joyful, positive movies. I see gratitude as the opposite of resentment. It can even serve as an antidote.

Just as you might suspect, keeping a gratitude journal promotes well-being. Yes, they've tested that too!

Another practice that helps immensely, of course, is Shamata. It's there that we can take a break from focusing on and reacting to outer stuff, and notice what's going on in our inner world. That's when we can best notice if there's a shrunken little corner of our hearts, in service of holding that grudge for George . . . or Mom . . . or whomever. I've done my own little experiments with gratitude in the course of teaching Shamata, and the vast majority of people have reported being much more capable of noticing these things right after doing Shamata than when just quietly thinking about them without Shamata first.

I'm not suggesting we just sweep unpleasant things under the rug. On the contrary, I'm advocating *resolving* them through the practice of forgiveness. Otherwise they'll lurk in the back (unconscious) or front (conscious) of your mind—either under the rug or on top of it. In either case the grievance is not resolved. Then once it's resolved we can follow through with letting go of the old habitual mind-movies and at first, consciously playing new ones until those become the new habit. At this point you might say, "Okay, okay, I'm sold on forgiveness. How do I actually *do* it?" That's what Dr. Luskin lays out so simply and clearly in his book, *Forgive for Good*.

If you're still not quite sure if you're ready to give up the grudge, or if you are, and are looking for a relatively short, simple way to do it, Luskin is your guy! His method, which he developed at Stanford University, was actually proven through numerous studies. One of those Stanford studies was on family members of people killed in the conflict in Northern Ireland. What a huge thing to forgive. If they were helped by this method, there's a pretty good chance you can use it to help yourself too. Once you've decided to go for it, it would help to land on a proven method from the start! In *Forgive for Good*, Dr. Luskin explains the method, provides the instructions used in the Stanford studies, and gives you the nine-step process to do for yourself. You can get an audio version of Luskin talking you through the steps, from Amazon.

While in that book he mostly focuses on people you might not see again, Dr. Luskin did a follow-up book for people who needed to forgive a spouse, called *Forgive for Love*. You could easily apply that latter book to any family relationship. In both marriage and family relationships—many friendships too—you want not only to resolve the hurt but also to have an ongoing, loving relationship with those who have hurt you.

Getting back to the problem of habitually watching miserable movies in the Netflix of our minds, I'm sure you've had the experience of suddenly realizing you've been spending most of an hour watching some bad inner movie, and conducting some miserable dialog with your wrongdoer. Shamata is a perfect way to be there to *notice* that we're watching a movie, and which one we've clicked on. Well, if you're like me, you might not notice, or be able to switch movies, right away. Before Shamata I was deep in those movies for stretches, followed by another and another ill-chosen movie without ever noticing or cutting them short. Through regular practice we can have more and more freedom to choose the movies we want to watch, rather than being led around by the nose by our habits. This applies not just to resentment but to all kinds of negative thoughts about ourselves, others, and life in general.

One lama put two piles of stones on his meditation table: a darker one on one side and a lighter one on the other. Whenever he noticed a negative thought, he put a dark stone in front. Whenever he noticed a positive one (such as any of the Four Boundless Qualities), he put a lighter one in front. At first there were at least as many darker stones as lighter ones, in front. Gradually, over time, there were fewer and fewer dark ones, and increasing numbers of lighter ones. Finally there were only lighter ones.

The highly respected Tibetan lama Bokar Rinpoche was a test subject for brain studies. He had no activity in the part of the brain on the right side, which is active when we experience negative emotions. The same area on the left side, associated with positive emotions, was all lit

SCIENCE TIDBIT

Shamata, the Boundless Qualities, and the Brain

Shamata also helps us to have the self-awareness, the meta-awareness—the true freedom—to choose a different movie. As I'd mentioned in Book 1, our brain's higher functions, such as the executive function, become stronger with regular Shamata practice. Also, the time gap between sensory input and our response becomes a bit bigger. From the point of view of our lived experience, it's like we have more moments of stepping back from the *story* of the movie and realizing we're in a theater, watching a movie. That feels like a key step to the freedom to choose. When we're sunk into the story, how can we even think to choose? This realization would help to explain why the Center for Healthy Minds suggests that meta-awareness is a *necessary* condition for transformation.[*]

In the Round Robin, we add in the Four Boundless Qualities that light up, among other regions, the left prefrontal cortex—the area in our brains associated with positive emotions. That combination of stronger executive function and a split-second gap in reaction time, along

[*]   Cortland J. Dahl, Christine D. Wilson-Mendenhall, and Richard J. Davidson, "The Plasticity of Well-Being: A Training-Based Framework for the Cultivation of Human Flourishing," *Proceedings of the National Academy of Sciences of the United States of America* 117, no. 51, 32197–32206. https://doi.org/10.1073/pnas.2014859117

up. The scientists, who at that time didn't yet know which parts of the brain lit up in association with what emotions, thought Bokar Rinpoche was sweet but maybe a bit of a simpleton. Now we know better.

Perhaps best of all, Shamata gives us a chance to take a break between movies, altogether. Many of us meditators report feeling inexpressible peace, happiness, and well-being while taking a moment to focus on something bigger than all those movies . . . looking up from Netflix for a moment . . . or at least noticing we're watching Netflix. This is why, when I'm meditating, I often like to pause even my breathing and savor a moment of deep, utter stillness.

While you may have done all of the above—applying Dr. Luskin's methods and doing Round Robin meditation—in some cases, such as

with bigger pathways to the more resourced parts of our brains, produces a wonderful result in how we respond to stimuli: instead of knee-jerk reactions from the primitive parts of our brains such as the amygdala (i.e. defense center), we respond from the more resourced parts of our brains. The Four Boundless Qualities together with Shamata, in time, help us to respond from the more advanced parts of our brains, bringing in the left prefrontal cortex.

When we pull ourselves out of those negative trains of thought to ones like the Four Boundless Qualities, we go from engaging the sympathetic nervous system (fight or flight) to the parasympathetic nervous system (rest and digest). And perhaps most importantly, we change our relationship to those negative thought-videos. Not only does all of that improve our blood pressure, heart rate variability, digestion, and immune system functions while lowering the risk for heart disease and cancer,* but it *feels good*. Shamata and the Four Boundless Qualities together, as in the Round Robin practice, give us as sure a route as any to change to positive movies. Again, this naturally affects our nervous system, and all the other above systems.

By alternating Shamata with one of the Four Boundless Qualities, not only do we change how our brains, nervous systems, and immune systems behave, but our outer behavior will also change as a natural reflection of our different thoughts and feelings.

---

* Luskin, Fred. *Forgive for Love: The Missing Ingredient for a Healthy and Lasting Relationship*. New York: HarperCollins, 2009, 32–33.

with a parent who had wronged you in your childhood, that person might still prove very difficult today. Actually, if *they've* been indulging negative movies in their minds all this time, they could be even more difficult these days. Of course you can't change them. Sometimes you doing your own part of the old dance differently evokes a different reaction from the other person. It's hard for them to behave in exactly the same way if you've changed the dance. Even so, there are some cases where, no matter how you're dancing, they're going to act in pretty much the same way. In that last case the most you can hope for is a more pleasant Thanksgiving dinner or an easier time at the occasional family wedding. But no matter what they're doing, now you're no longer adding to your own pain by carrying the hot coals of resentment into the room. That's nothing to sneeze at!

This brings us to the subject of Dr. Luskin's follow-up book, *Forgive for Love*, which I mentioned briefly earlier. Let's face it, in all relationships we need to be able to forgive (and, I might add, need to be forgiven). Everyone makes mistakes, and on top of that, we don't always agree on what a mistake is. Life at close range with our beloveds is going to give us ongoing opportunities to choose between forgiveness and grudge-nursing. It has to be one or the other—even if you try to pretend something doesn't bother you. If by "never mind" you mean, "I don't want to deal with this so I'll just sweep it under the rug," what you're really saying is, "I'll just hold this grudge in secret." Sure, in the moment it seems easier, but I'm sure you can see how this can wear away at your loving connection. And I'm not just talking of sweethearts or life partners. I'm talking between parents and children, roommates, business partners, and any other relationships at close range. How does it work for you if someone you're close to is secretly holding a grudge?

There's yet one more person to practice forgiveness with, perhaps the most important one of all: yourself. That might also be the most difficult. Yet how can you forgive others if you don't forgive yourself? That's as hard as loving others when you don't love yourself. Again, Dr. Luskin has worked with that difficult task of forgiving yourself. And just as with others, forgiving yourself doesn't mean justifying, or forgetting (and thus not learning from), your own mistakes; it means letting go of your own resentment, and grudges, toward yourself.

Carl Jung would say that forgiveness does far more than make family relationships, business relationships, marriages, and your relationships better, though. That hard work you do in the depths of your heart is work you do for us all. Of course there's the idea that if everyone did as you did, the world would be a much better place. But that's not how Jung meant it. You might remember Rupert Sheldrake's work that I talked about in Book 1. The more people learn something, the more quickly the next people learn it. Though Sheldrake has been doing his work after Jung's death, I think they're both pointing to something in the same direction—like the principle of modern physics that recognizes whatever causes the phenomenon of twin particles that move and change simultaneously, even at a distance.

Jung saw the universe as deeply connected, perhaps similar to a hologram. Remember the David Bohm Science Tidbit in Book 1 titled "Holomovement"? I don't think Jung read Bohm's work on Holomovement, but he had a similar understanding of how our minds and the universe are related to each other. He also believed that the world was on the cusp of possible destruction. In fact, he had visions of it. He firmly believed that if we were going to avert such an end, it would happen through enough people reaching "individuation"—i.e. waking up out of our common dream of reality. Remember, "buddha" means "one who is awake."

NOBODY'S ASKING YOU TO BE A DOORMAT!

You might be wondering if Buddhist thought advocates being a doormat. Not at all! To pick an example on the world stage, Thich Nhat Hanh, the famous Vietnamese Buddhist master, was a passionate activist against the Vietnam War. Tibetan Buddhism in general gives us wonderful guidance in how to bring out the fiercer parts of ourselves when it's appropriate. You might have seen images of ferocious beings with long eyeteeth, brandishing weapons and looking perfectly ready to use them. They're enlightened beings who usually can also appear in peaceful forms . . . but if another being is causing harm and won't respond to peaceful attempts, they can readily protect their wrathful forms.

They aren't pissed off, in the common way that you and I would be. Being enlightened—coming from the point of view of the whole ocean—they want to spare not only the sentient beings who could be harmed, but also the harmdoer. It's much like a mother dog snarling and nipping one of her puppies when they wander into trouble. We practice wrathful deities to evoke that archetype in ourselves, and

Pema Traktung, a wrathful form of Guru Rinpoche, who protects us especially from modern diseases, but really any kind. Totally enlightened and full of compassion. Totally fierce!

to develop that particular capacity. During the practice we're even to experience *ourselves* to be that being. I've been Pema Traktung many times! Carl Jung believed we all have all of the archetypes within us. Since they're principles of reality, therefore pervading all reality, where *wouldn't* they be? So it really helped me to embody my own assertive Pema Traktung from within . . . and to bring that powerful universal archetype to bear on various fronts, inner and outer.

On a more mundane, personal level, in a moment when someone has done something hurtful to you, if you can give them constructive feedback so that hurtful thing they did won't happen again, that's good preventive medicine. Even after the fact, sometimes it's just good to let someone know they've hurt you—especially in a close relationship, especially if they may not realize how what they've done has affected you. Again, this can be preventive medicine for future friction. My favorite form of giving such feedback is a method called Nonviolent Communication (NVC).* It works, mainly because it turns out that if you're clear and kind in speaking to them about it, and stick with *your own* feelings rather than telling them about *them*, the person is more apt to accept your feedback rather than getting into a shouting match with you.

When I first came upon NVC, I had to work to practice the steps, trying to apply them to various situations where I needed to give someone difficult feedback. It was easier for me to do it in written form then, such as an email. If I forgot a step or needed to correct it, I could. As I kept practicing, in trainings and then mostly in life (since life seems generous with steady opportunities to say "ouch" to people), I got skilled enough that I could apply the principles more naturally and seamlessly, live and in person. I can say for sure that this has helped me to be happier and kinder. I'm sure they have no idea, but sometimes I think, "If only you knew how relieved you should be that I'm practicing NVC!"

---

* For a brief introduction from the founder of Nonviolent Communication, Marshall Rosenberg, here's a nine-minute introduction he gives on YouTube: https://www.youtube.com/watch?v=M-129JLTjkQ Or just go to YouTube and type "The Basics of Nonviolent Communication 1.1" into the search field.

ANOTHER KIND OF PREVENTIVE MEDICINE
Sometimes, as with that person who cut you off in traffic and gave you the One Finger Salute, NVC is not the right preventive medicine. You can save yourself a whole lot of forgiveness work if you don't even take in that stuff in the first place. In *The Law of the Garbage Truck**, author David J. Pollay gives us clear, simple ways to identify when someone is trying to dump their garbage on our doorstep, and exactly how to avoid taking it personally and thereby taking it in. He applies it to a surprising number of relationships and situations. (He also avoids the simplistic mistake of missing true feedback which we'd be wise to accept—not every criticism or "negative" observation is garbage!) In the area of preventive medicine, you could save yourself (and by association, others) a whole lot of hurt, mess, and needing to do a bunch of forgiveness, by becoming skilled at not allowing other people's garbage in.

Every once in a while I could've done better.

To paraphrase the old saying: "Everyone's wrong but thee and me. And sometimes I wonder about thee." We've all been in relationships when at times we WISHED that So-and-So would just admit they're wrong so everybody could move on. But if you get *near* talking about their mistake they get defensive and nasty, making it all even worse.

Are we SURE it's everyone *else* who does that? Might we sometimes? As you might remember, I've talked about the "I'm Sorry" Practice that I invented for myself when I was in my twenties. I challenged myself to admit I was wrong about something at least once a day. Instead of feeling embarrassed, I'd give myself an inner pat on the back for being brave. At first it was scary. I thought I'd look like a fool. But I quickly found out the opposite. The other person already knew I'd made the mistake, and the bullshitting and/or defensiveness only made me look worse. The other person was relieved when I admitted I was wrong, and especially if I apologized. And I learned something from admitting the mistake—surprise! Even more often, I find myself admitting I could've handled some interaction better. I sure appreciate it when the other person does! And again, I learn a lot. I now believe that human relations could be so much simpler if

---

*   Pollay, David J. *The Law of the Garbage Truck: How to Stop People from Dumping on You,* New York: Sterling Publishing Co., Inc., 2012.

everybody just admitted when they were wrong and/or could've done something better.

Which brings us to a big question: WHEN do we decide somebody's trying to dump their garbage at our feet and we shouldn't accept it, and when might there be at least a grain of truth? Here's another question: even if the other person isn't dumping anything, might we be resenting them for not living up to our expectations? Who hasn't felt that? But if we're willing to turn the lens inward, we might discover that the person responsible for unfulfilled expectations was the one doing the expecting.

> If we're willing to turn the lens inward, we might discover that the person responsible for unfulfilled expectations was the one doing the expecting.

I think one reason we're so afraid to take responsibility for our mistakes is that in our society we're trained to pass judgment on people for their actions . . . and judge ourselves most harshly of all. We can evaluate *actions* as mistaken or not—which I think is helpful and necessary—or perfect or in need of improvement, but we don't then have to judge the *person* to be essentially unworthy. If we do Shamata and the Boundless Qualities, we're sitting in the experience of that ocean/waves essential reality. THAT's who we all are. So whatever we *do* doesn't change the fact that we're made of that pure water. Just *imagine* if everyone in the world could make that clear distinction between the action and the person.

As you practice Boundless Equanimity and Boundless Loving Kindness, I hope you study and learn the forgiveness, NVC, and Garbage Truck skills and apply them so you can truly practice those Boundless Qualities even for the troublemakers in your life. And by practicing those along with Shamata, I'm sure you'll grow your capacity to know what part you might have in a problem (or not),

> Just *imagine* if everyone in the world could make that clear distinction between the action and the person.

and more skillfully navigate through it. May your capacity of heart grow boundlessly, and may you come into right connection with all and everyone . . . not least of all . . . *yourself.*

BOUNDLESS
(IMMEASURABLE) COMPASSION

The next Boundless Quality is Compassion. I've said a whole lot about that already, in Book 2, and you already have an excellent method for practicing it—Tonglen. What more could there be to say?

Well, a little. Okay: maybe a fair amount. I want to share a couple of stories that always touch me. I think of this first one when I feel overwhelmed with strong compassion. Sometimes all we feel we can do is sit and cry. And sometimes that is just the thing to do. Joanna Macy, a famous Buddhist environmentalist/activist, believes that if we bury/hide from our grief over the world, we won't be energized to get up and DO something about it. When I look at the need for action in the world, and how many of us go about our days without doing much, I can see her point. Sometimes grief is appropriate.

One time a monk came to visit Geshe Tönpa. The monk knew four others that Geshe Tönpa had trained: three brothers, as well as another fellow named Khampa Lungpa. Wanting to catch up on the news, Geshe Tönpa asked, "What is Potowa doing these days?" He was one of the three brothers.

"He is teaching hundreds of people all of the time," replied the monk.

"Oh, that's so good to hear! Have you heard any news of Geshe Puchungwa?" He was another of the three brothers.

"As a matter of fact I have. He is constantly making beautiful statues, paintings, and other representations of the Buddha."

"That's also good to hear," smiled Geshe Tönpa. "And Gönpawa? What's he up to?"

"He only meditates all day—nothing else."

"How wonderful! And what about Khampa Lhungpa? Do you know what he's doing these days?"

"Well, I'm sorry to tell you, he just sits alone all day with his prayer shawl over his head, weeping at the suffering of beings."

At that, Geshe Tönpa took off his hat, put his hands together in front of his heart and began to cry deeply. When he regained his voice, he said, "This is the best news of all. He's *really* practicing the Dharma. I could go on and on about his great qualities, but I know he wouldn't want me to."

STUDENT *Is it really just enough to cry and pray? Don't we need to do something about the suffering in the world?*

LT I can't speak for Geshe Tönpa, but I have some thoughts from listening to various masters and thinking a lot about this myself. I'm not being facetious but totally serious when I say "both/and." First of all, we each have our own talents and leanings, not to mention karmic leanings and opportunities. Some people are very persuasive people and can change the world, the way Bill Wilson and Bob Smith did in starting Alcoholics Anonymous. Through the brave and strategic efforts of many demonstrators and media people, the war in Vietnam was stopped. I mentioned Joanna Macy, who has spent most of her nine decades working tirelessly and strategically to ward off the worst environmental disasters. The Buddha was a gifted teacher but he didn't stop there. In his time, he single-handedly started a movement that ended the caste system for many centuries. It's worth mentioning that at another time in his life, all he did was meditate for years at a time.

Which brings me to an important point. Sometimes it's time to do inner work; sometimes to work in our close community; sometimes to be active in the larger world. Without inner work, our relationships will probably suffer. Without healthy community, we're probably not going to be as effective out in the world. We may not even pick the best strategies for outer work without doing inner work. Around and around it goes; those three areas supporting each other, forging a satisfyingly meaningful life.

STUDENT *So are you saying that a meditation retreat would make me a better activist?*

LT And vice versa! Inner work (including perhaps, some psychology) will help you aim your outer efforts better, fueled by wisdom and compassion rather than by old frustrations disguised as righteous causes. And the outer work will bring merit (positive karma and habits of mind) that will help you on the cushion. I've believed this for a long time, based on my own experience, so I was happy to hear Rinpoche say the same thing. Working on the community level helps in both directions because we learn a lot about ourselves in community. In the outer direction, we have exponentially more power to change the world if we do it in healthy partnership with others. And I don't know of many people who have sustained a meditation practice without doing it in community sometimes too.

The Story of Asanga

Here's another story that shows how you can clean your karmic windshield not only through Shamata but through the bodhicitta approach of Boundless Compassion. Remember, whatever transforms our karmic and habitual tendency toward self-centeredness removes obscurations from our lens—our windshield. It takes a lot of repetition to transform habits, creating and expanding new neural pathways, and dissolving the old ones.

Long ago, in ancient India, a Dharma student named Asanga had a goal: to see the Future Buddha Maitreya, who was already a great bodhisattva. He then planned on getting instructions from him.

He began a Maitreya practice retreat in a cave on Kukkutapada Mountain. Asanga spent all his waking hours, every single day, reciting Maitreya's mantra, visualizing him, making offerings to him and so on. This went on for six years. He never saw Maitreya, even in his dreams. No sign of any kind. Nothing. He became discouraged and gave up.

After completing the closing rituals for his retreat, he packed up his things and walked down the road in despair. He came upon a man rubbing a huge iron pole with a soft cloth.

"What are you doing, my friend?" Asanga asked.

"I need a needle, so I'm rubbing this pole, to fashion it into a needle."

"Hmmm," thought Asanga, "It would take him a century of rubbing to do the job. Yet he's persevering. Here I am, supposedly a good practitioner, and I've quit my lofty goal after only six years. And my goal is way more important and beneficial than a needle could ever be." He was embarrassed, regretful that he didn't know the meaning of persistence. He turned around and went back to the cave.

For three more years he did nothing else but pray to Maitreya continuously. Still no sign whatsoever. This time he was *positive* that there was absolutely no hope of seeing Maitreya, that he was wasting his life, accomplishing nothing. Again, he ended retreat, packed up his few possessions, and walked down the path.

The first person he came upon was a man at the foot of a towering rock. The man was dipping a feather in water and stroking the rock. "What are you trying to do here?" Asanga asked, more than a little bewildered. "This rock is blocking the sunlight from my house, so I'm wearing it away," the man explained.

Immediately Asanga's mind went to the thoughts of three years before, and he returned to the cave, practicing with renewed vigor. Three years passed. Nothing, nada, zilch.

"That's it!" he declared, now in complete despair. "No matter what I do, I see that if I do this for a million years, I'll get nowhere." He packed up his things and left for good.

This time he didn't come upon any men doing bizarre things. He did come upon a dog, however. Her two hind legs were crippled, and she pulled herself along in the most painful way. Her hindquarters were covered with writhing maggots. Somehow she managed to find the strength to bite any hand that came near. Asanga was overcome with the most unbearable wave of compassion. His heart would break if he couldn't help her.

But how? When he got near her, she snarled and tried to bite his hand. He could see that on top of everything else, she was starving. Without a thought, he cut off a piece of his own flesh and fed it to her. Clearly his years of meditating on the great, compassionate Bodhisattva Matraiya hadn't been a waste. Would we have the compassion to feed our flesh to an ill-tempered, rotting dog? Then he turned his attention to the maggots. He didn't see how he could pick them off of her without crushing their mushy little bodies. But he felt compassion for them too. The only thing he could think of to use was, well, his tongue. He couldn't bear to lick them off if he looked at the maggots, so he closed his eyes and bent down to begin.

His tongue touched the ground.

He opened his eyes. No dog. He looked up.

There was the huge, glowing Bodhisattva Maitreya! Asanga felt the force of his power and love pouring out in all directions. The first thing he thought of to say was, "Maitreya! Where have you *been* all these years! I've been praying to you, visualizing you, saying your mantra, and you never appeared in all that time!"

Maitreya smiled, "Asanga, I was there with you every single minute. And when you gave up, I appeared as the man with the scarf, the man with the feather, and now a dog."

Asanga wept at the thought. "But . . . but . . ."

"You couldn't see me because of your own past negative actions and obscurations. Over all those years, you cleared away *almost* enough of them, so that I appeared as a festering dog. Your act of compassion

Maitreya, who is said to be the next Buddha

finally cleared away enough, and made your vision pure enough that you could see me."

"No! That's impossible. Anyone could see you the way you're appearing now. You're huge and glowing, and clear as day!"

"If you don't believe me, let's go into town and find out if anyone else can see me."

Asanga wasn't convinced, so they went to the nearby village. Asanga carried Maitreya on his right shoulder. He asked everyone at the market what they saw. Every one of them looked at him a little strangely and said they saw nothing. At last they came to an old woman at the edge of town, whose obscurations were relatively more cleared away than the villagers'. When Asanga asked her, she said, "The rotting corpse of a dog."

After that, Maitreya took Asanga to a pure realm and gave him the very high teachings that he had so fervently prayed for. Asanga went on to become one of the greatest Buddhist masters of ancient India. He's still famous today. His works are still studied, and he still inspires thousands of people. I've just told you his story, and you've now just read it, so the benefit of all of Asanga's hard work is still rippling out.

This story reminds us that, in training in bodhicitta in general, and Compassion in particular, we can accomplish the two processes that lead toward enlightenment: clearing away obscurations, and bringing forth our Buddha Nature. You can see why Compassion is essential to Mahayana and Vajrayana Buddhism.

Even though buddhas and great bodhisattvas can appear anywhere, even in the *Bardo* (the dreamlike state between lifetimes) or our dreams, if we're too caught in our own fixations and obscurations, we can't see them. And even if we do see something, we can't see these beings as they really are. When we see with the eyes of compassion, we see more truly.

Long before we ever get within a mile of enlightenment, we can see our loved ones, co-workers, and others with purer vision and more open hearts. I remember talking with one longtime Dharma student who shook his head and mused, "After practicing Dharma, we can master worldly life . . . but by then that's not our goal." He was pointing to the fact that we get better at worldly life after all this practice, but by that time what we really want to do is to wake up *out* of it, altogether.

Springtime at the Namchak Retreat Ranch

BOUNDLESS (IMMEASURABLE) SYMPATHETIC JOY

This one is a nice balance to the previous Boundless Quality, Compassion. After you've done a lot of Tonglen, it's refreshing— and I recommend it—to practice Sympathetic Joy. Now, instead of *suffering*-with, you get to be *joyful*-with! It's really still about feeling the truth of your underlying non-separateness from others.

As with the other Boundless Qualities, GET SPECIFIC. That's the best way I know to keep it real. If your thinking is vague, your feelings will be too. Pick someone and something specific (a dear friend getting over a terrible disease, someone's vocational success, the birth of a relative's child, friendship, knowledge, art, the bonds within a particular community . . . anything you wish) to feel joyful about. You might keep that particular theme, as you step it out to others, in that day's practice. As ever, start with yourself, or one very close to you and then yourself, and go out from there. At first you might pick specific people, then eventually whole categories of beings. Then share joy with, yes, those who cause you trouble. Eventually you're sympathetically joyful for all beings everywhere. At some time or another, they've all had moments of joy, and will again. Since linear time is an illusion, be happy with them now. In the process, wish them even more joy, as soon as possible. Then feel into that, and feel your own joy in sympathy with theirs.

Let's get specific, right now, with this particular Boundless Quality. For example, you may be feeling really happy from a recent visit with your old friend. You had a really good talk or two. How lucky, that you have such a friend, that you can feel the closeness that comes from having shared so much together. You imagine hugging each other hello, basking in that love. As you sit in that warm feeling, allow yourself to savor and celebrate it. "I just had a great visit with Dave!" Under that focus, the feeling of joy will probably grow quite naturally.

For starters you can extend that feeling to Dave, who probably also feels joy about your visit. You're equally happy for him. Lucky guy!

Now you think of someone else you know and love, who also has that same feeling of closeness with someone they love (but this time, not you). You imagine their smiling face as they meet with their loved one. You could imagine them hugging. You can't help but smile in Sympathetic Joy. Now you see more people you know, feeling connected with their loved ones. You celebrate that connection for each and all of them.

Then you let the tide of Sympathetic Joy roll out to the next ring. You imagine whole classes of beings feeling the joy of connection: mother dogs with their puppies, licking each other on the mouth (ew!) in joyful reunion after the mother was gone for a few minutes. They *love* it! You smile at their joy. Then the tide of Joy rolls out to lovers . . . then all mothers and babies . . . fathers and babies . . . as many groups as you can think of. Your heart is positively *glowing* with Joy!

If you feel ready, you could next push the envelope a little, and imagine someone who's caused you problems. They must have friends and family they love too. They're bound to feel joy when they meet them after being away. Imagine them hugging their loved one, smiling, laughing. Now that you have this big tide of Sympathetic Joy going, you can feel Joy in Sympathy with them, just for this thing, just in this moment. In this moment, they're simply another sentient being, and they're feeling joy. In this moment, that's all that matters. This is a good time to again remember what Neem Karoli Baba said: "Never throw anyone out of your heart." It accomplishes nothing but making your own heart smaller. That's a big price to pay for indulging—yes, indulging—in feeling righteous (and almost all our feelings of righteousness are really *self*-righteousness). Let your heart expand and allow it to feel real Joy in this being's joy.

Now you can extend that Joy to all sentient beings. At one time or another, they all have felt that joy of meeting with a loved one.

STUDENT   *Am I supposed to feel Sympathetic Joy for someone who's happy they've hurt someone, or done some bad deed?*

LT   No. There's plenty that's positive to be Sympathetically Joyful about. We've all done terrible things and we're are all happy to be hugged by someone we love. We all are happy to eat a good meal, or behold a beautiful sight, listen to our favorite music, help someone, get a hug from a loved one, or just to take a good rest after a long day. We can pick those kinds of things, which are pretty universal. Also, remember that you are probably expanding outward from your own feelings of joy: if you felt joy at hurting someone or doing a bad deed, you would have some work ahead of you!

NEAR AND FAR ENEMIES

In working with the Four Boundless Qualities, we need to take care not to detour into other, drastically different states, accidentally cultivating them instead, or into the even more dangerous apparently similar states. They will lead us away from our goal of feeling our connection with others, rather than toward it. Buddhism refers to Far Enemies (opposite qualities) and Near Enemies (imposters that could still lead us away from connection).

The Buddha spoke of both a Near and Far Enemy for each of the Boundless Qualities, and there are some first cousins to those enemies that we might want to look at too.

Each of the Four Boundless Qualities gets us past our ego fixation and *joins* us with another being, in a way that brings right relationship.

We can feel that rightness and joining when it happens. And, as we know from neuroscience, that feeling registers in that ever-popular left middle prefrontal lobe, a main locus of positive emotions. From a Buddhist point of view, it's bringing forth our Buddha Nature by expanding that aspect of it that knows we're not separate. Again, the Four Boundless Qualities bring forth that awareness through *feeling,* as opposed to some other practices like Insight Meditation. In In*sight* Meditation, we *see* how we're not separate—also important, and Insight Meditation dovetails perfectly with practices such as the Boundless Qualities. That's why we do them together in the Round Robin Practice.

The Far Enemy of a Boundless Quality is an opposite quality, which has an obvious separating effect, certainly an enemy to the goal of feeling joined with others. It's generally easier to catch ourselves falling into the Far Enemy than the Near because the difference is so dramatic and obvious. Unless we're going out of our way to fool ourselves, it would be difficult to mistake a Far Enemy for its opposite Boundless Quality. We can get distracted (as ever) in our meditation and not notice it at first, but an emotion such as hate is pretty nasty looking

once we're awake enough to notice. Of course, Shamata helps us to get better and better at catching such feelings earlier.

A Near Enemy doesn't look so obviously nasty, so we might see it and mistake it for the Boundless Quality we're trying to practice. As Hamlet notes, "The devil hath power to assume a pleasing shape." The Near Enemy, dressed up like a Boundless Quality, has a more subtle separating effect. This makes the Near Enemy more dangerous than the Far, because we can go on for hours and hours thinking we're cultivating an Boundless Quality, and congratulating ourselves, when in fact we're becoming more and more habituated to a separating quality of mind.

Equanimity: Near and Far Enemies

Let's start with Equanimity. This seems distinct and clear enough. We practice Equanimity to expand our feeling of warm, caring connection to all beings, equally strong for every one of them. Its Far Enemy is an equally clear opposite. It's that Buddhist classic, Attraction/Aversion—in other words, Preference. If we feel preference for some people over others—*my* brother, *my* friend, *my* ally—we're obviously not practicing Equanimity. And if we are annoyed, angered, repulsed by some people, then we're obviously not practicing Equanimity, either.

Of course we all *do* feel preferences for some people over others. We feel attraction and love for some, and aversion toward others. This just means that we're not buddhas yet, and we could do with some Boundless Equanimity practice. The good news is that it's fairly obvious that when we're feeling this Far Enemy we're, well, far away from Equanimity. By definition, any of the Boundless Qualities and its Far Enemy can't co-exist in our minds. They're opposites. So as long as we feel Preference, we're clearly not feeling Boundless Equanimity, and vice versa.

Sometimes in my psychotherapy practice, a client would insult or accuse me during a therapy session. I could handle it with equanimity; after the session I didn't think about it again. Though I certainly cared about the person—I came to love every one of my clients—I wasn't feeling strong Desire or Aversion toward them. On the other hand, if a family member or enemy were to say the same thing, I might very well be hurt or furious. The incident would live on in my head, causing me consternation every time I thought about it. And if someone I am especially close to does something particularly nice for me, I may feel more strongly motivated to nurture their well-being than I am the well-being of the ones who insulted me.

As we all know, love and hate are very close: intense feelings toward someone who is a central figure in our mental and emotional landscape. In either case—feeling hate toward anyone, or feeling love to the exclusion of, and to the detriment of, others—we would be in the territory of the Far Enemy of Equanimity. The loss of Equanimity was brought on by the Desire or Aversion driving us to express our anger or our gratitude. Though this Far Enemy can be a real struggle to work with, its advantage is that at least it's obvious.

Not so with Equanimity's Near Enemy. If we consider its Near Enemy for a minute, I think you'll be able to remember seeing it mistaken for Equanimity in others and . . . yes, even yourself.

The Near Enemy is less dramatic and less obvious. The Near Enemy of Equanimity is Indifference. You can fall into it and stay there for a long time, rather smug that you're feeling Equanimity . . . but you're not.

Indifference is dressed in Equanimity's "clothing," but it feels different. It also has a different effect. "I don't care" is not the same as "I care deeply, equally, and inclusively."

Until his Christmas Eve epiphany, Ebenezer Scrooge treated everyone with equal indifference (he didn't care that it was Christmas, he didn't care that Tiny Tim was ill, he didn't care that his long-time business partner had died, he didn't care about the poor), but he wasn't practicing Equanimity.

That's still rather obvious, but there are much less obvious examples. How many times have you found yourself or others feeling pleased to not be upset by someone else's angst? Or perhaps in our Equanimity practice, we notice we don't lean too far toward the people we prefer, congratulating ourselves on our restraint. If we look closely, though, we might be practicing Indifference rather than Equanimity. The exercise has become theoretical, and *feeling* is lost altogether. Though it can look like Equanimity, Indifference serves to separate us from the objects of our Indifference rather than connect us in strong feelings of love.

Let's take the practice of Tonglen, for example. In this case, Equanimity means feeling *equally Compassionate* toward whomever we're thinking of (and as you'll recall, by the end of the practice, we're usually thinking quite inclusively). The word "compassion" itself, from the Latin, literally means, "to suffer with."

When we start Tonglen practice, we develop the strong, passionate desire to take away the loved one's suffering and replace it with ultimate, lasting joy. The feeling is so strong that we're sometimes in tears (though often smiling at the same time, as we bring them ultimate, lasting happiness on the outbreath). Then we step *that same compassionate feeling* out to *all beings*, thus bringing Compassion together with Equanimity. This is what makes it a *Boundless* (instead of measured, bounded, or limited) Quality. This is hardly Indifference. But beware, because Indifference can creep into your practice in all of the Four Boundless Qualities, not just with Compassion. That is exactly why the Buddha emphasized this distinction.

In order for any of the Four Boundless Qualities to be truly beyond measure, we have to feel each of them intensely, and without bias. That's why Rinpoche always tells us to *practice Equanimity first.* I apply it to all the Boundless Qualities while I'm practicing them, stepping the rings out to include all sentient beings. That's why I begin close in, to those for whom I can easily feel strongly. That primes the pump of caring and connection, and helps protect me from falling into Indifference. That allows my Love and Compassion to roll out strongly to all beings, with equal force. My feeling of loving connection increasingly approaches Boundless.

Imagine if we all felt as much love and compassion for everyone as we do for our best friend. How would the world look? Really play that out in your mind right now.

Now imagine what would happen to your own tight grip on your identity—your ego—if you felt that strongly for everyone. How would you then feel about giving your spot in the checkout line to someone who seemed to be in even more of a hurry than you were?

STUDENT   *If compassion means "suffering with," how is it different from "empathy"?*

LT   According to the Chambers Dictionary, empathy means "the power of entering into another's personality and imaginatively experiencing his or her experiences." We certainly need the capacity to empathize, in order to be compassionate, but compassion goes further. When we feel compassion for someone, we not only "feel their pain," but we have the strong desire to remove that pain and to see them happy. Remember that the *breathing in the darkness and pain* part in Tonglen is followed immediately and inevitably by the *breathing out happiness* part of Tonglen. We're moved to a positive *response* by their suffering, not just wallowing in it along with them.

If we only experience empathy, we could be led around by the nose, experiencing whatever the other person is feeling—happy or sad or angry or lost—and not feel like doing anything about it. In that case nobody benefits. Empathy alone can be rather dissatisfying, in my experience. Compassion brings us into a sense of connection that *feels right*. This is a clue that we're in right relationship with the other.

During my time as a psychotherapist, sometimes a client would tell me about an event weighted with such suffering that I wanted to collapse into a puddle of tears. That's certainly *suffering with*, but it was not going to benefit my client. Contrary to the popular saying, misery doesn't really love company—misery would really rather be transformed into happiness. I needed to empathize and suffer with the client enough to be deeply in the experience with them, but also keep

> Jumping into the swirling river with someone
> who is drowning is an empathetic gesture—
> but tossing them a lifeline from the riverbank
> would probably be more compassionate.

one foot "on shore," so to speak, so that I could lead them to some sort of learning and healing. Jumping into the swirling river with someone who is drowning is an empathetic gesture—but tossing them a lifeline from the riverbank would probably be more compassionate.

Those moments required walking a fine line, but even though I sometimes shed tears with them, my intention to be of benefit helped me not to indulge the wallowing. Again, intention is key.

Loving Kindness: Near and Far Enemies

The obvious opposite to Loving Kindness is Hatred, or its little brother, Ill Will. I hardly think you need an explanation of that one. Of course the *ability* to dispense with Ill Will isn't as easy as recognizing it when you see, or feel, it. That's what the practice is for.

The classic Near Enemy to Loving Kindness is Sentimentality. Until my Buddhist training, I hadn't heard that, but as soon as I did, I realized "Aha! That's exactly right!" Somehow we do know that, while Loving Kindness joins us in right relationship with another, *Sentimentality subtly separates us.* It's more self-referential, and in the wave of Sentimentality we bathe ourselves in, we've lost sight of the presumed object of our feelings—the other human being. They've become a screen for our own maudlin movie.

I have a dear childhood friend who's VERY sentimental about everything, pretty constantly. She's afloat in a sea of Sentimentality and revels in being carried about on its waves and tides. She's been an extremely loyal friend through the years, but when I talk to her of my life and she swoons over some little thing I've mentioned, I don't feel her love for me. It doesn't feel like she's responding to *me,* and I find no satisfaction or sense of joining, in talking to her about my circumstances. Sad but true.

Instead I feel like she's doing two things: using me to pat herself on the back for being a loving friend, and indulging in surges of drama, using my story almost like a TV show. "Using" being the operative word. TV shows are meant to entertain the audience. That's what I feel I provide for her. No wonder visits with her feel less than satisfying for me. I believe that, if she practiced true Loving Kindness, she would feel much more satisfied too, because she would feel truly connected to her friend. Unfortunately, since she's not able or even particularly willing to change this habit, I love her *despite* the Sentimentality, not *in response to* Loving Kindness.

STUDENT *I'm still not quite getting this. Isn't "sentiment" the same as "feeling"? And "feeling" is good, right?*

LT You're right that being able to feel for, and with, others is important—essential, even. For example, when you feel true sympathetic joy for someone else's happiness, or sorrow for their grief, you are feeling with that particular person. The same is true for Loving Kindness: you feel it for a particular person (or being)—even if it's for *all* individuals.

But sentimentality is generic. Some people feel sentimental about puppies—any puppy—or weddings, in general, no matter who is getting married—fictional characters, even!

And sentimentality is also self-involved, burrowing inward rather than reaching out.

STUDENT   *So if I'm mostly aware of me, it's not true Loving Kindness.*

LT   Exactly. It's like in the Beatles' song "She's Leaving Home," when instead of being happy for their daughter's independence, or even worrying about her safety, the mother's reaction is "How could she do this to me?"

Let me give you a real example. A few years ago, a colleague's wife died, and a couple of days before her death, a teenage friend of the family left her a voice-mail, even though he knew she had by then drifted into unconsciousness. My friend's therapist later described the message as "heartfelt, but not at all sentimental." Here's part of what the voicemail said—notice that it's about, and for, the particular person, facing outward, toward her spirit.

"I'm just calling because I want to say I love you, and I want to thank you for everything you've done for my mom, for me, for my brother and sisters. You had a very adventurous spirit, and I was glad to be a part of it. I'm glad I got to know it, and I'm glad I got to see it and the shell that it was in, which was yours. I'll never forget you—your smiling face, your endearing nature, and the caring individual you are, and will always be, and we'll always remember you by. Again, I know you can't say it back, but I want to let you know that I can still hear you say it. I love you very much. Bye."

Another Near Enemy is Conditional Love, a prevalent form of which—desire/clinging—is easily and often mistaken for true Love. The most popular arena for this little substitution is in romantic love. Especially during the first three years of a relationship, huge loads of endorphins, the pleasure chemical in our brains, are produced. (Many "recreational drugs" artificially trigger them—making them hard to resist and hard to abandon.) Endorphins are the original high, and we can stimulate them naturally with new romantic love. Of course we'd desire as much of that as we can get, and cling to every opportunity. But even without the brain science you knew that. As soon as I mention desire/clinging being mistaken for love, I'm sure you can think of examples in your own life.

In my early adult years, I was terribly guilty of this one. It wasn't even just the rush of the endorphins, for me. On top of that, I was still looking for the lost warmth and closeness from my dad—I didn't get as much as I wanted because he was working so much and traveled a lot for his work. Once that early stage of life passes, we can never fully make up for the missing critical pieces. That sure doesn't stop us from trying, though. Again and again and again. Of course we're never satisfied. And of course the other person recoils from our clinginess. I saw this happen more than once, in my own life, but couldn't stop myself. At first I didn't even realize that my very clinging was driving the person away. It's perhaps ironic that we all want to be needed, but we find *neediness* unappealing.

Much later, I found myself on the other end of the stick. My boyfriend at the time—we'll call him Ralph—was extremely affectionate. But when we were with other people, if I looked at someone as they were talking to me, he'd go into a jealous sulk and afterward give me a long lecture about how I'd ignored and slighted him. When friends were visiting, he would sometimes literally pout in the corner. He hated my going on retreats and complained bitterly every time. If I traveled for work, he wanted to come with me, though there was no reason for him to come. If he had actually been feeling Love, he would have been happy to see me doing retreat, which benefited me so deeply. As it was, I felt oppressed. As you might expect, I pulled away. Ralph's feelings toward me felt like Attachment, not Love. I felt like I was his stuffed animal. While he was sure that he was intensely, deeply loving me, I felt he was practicing Attachment with great fervor.

Important warning for practicing this method: I'd mentioned before that we Westerners might need to start with Loving Kindness for *ourselves*. This too, has a Near Enemy: self-centeredness. We've already got that one *down*. (As I once heard someone remark wryly, "I'm not much. But I'm all I ever think about.") But it's not the same as the universal, spacious, powerful Loving Kindness that we've been talking about. Instead of "Love thy neighbor as thyself," it becomes, "Love thyself at the expense of thy neighbor," or "Love thyself, who cares about thy neighbor?" Oops. It seems to me that some people practicing and promoting pop psychology or "life coaching" fall into this. Not exactly what the Buddha was encouraging.

The acid test for any of the Near Enemies is to see if it causes us to be more, or less, empathetic with fellow sentient beings; does it join us or part us? And self-centeredness, of course, is exactly what the whole of Buddhism is trying to help us out of.

Compassion: Near and Far Enemies

Let's next turn our attention to Compassion. The obvious opposite feeling, the Far Enemy of Compassion, would be Cruelty. I don't think I have to explain to you how Hitler and his friends were practicing something as far away from Compassion as possible. (It's worth noting, by the way, that a lot of the less zealous "everyday" Nazis were practicing the Near Enemy of Equanimity, Indifference; they didn't care what was happening around them, in their name.)

The Near Enemy of Compassion is Pity. As with the other Near Enemies, we can absolutely feel the difference on the receiving end. No one likes to be pitied, but we all appreciate Compassion. Why is that? Pity puts the recipient in a one-down position—by definition breaching the goal of Equanimity. It disrespects them. If I've had a terrible accident and am in a wheelchair, I'm not comforted by someone saying, "There there, you *poor thing.*" I'd be inspired to heal just enough to stand up and smack them!

Someone coming from genuine Compassion would be sensitive to what would feel good to *me*. They might ask me what I'd like, offer to get me something, or even just talk to me about something other than my condition. When I broke my foot, I could feel such people's warmth, caring, and *respect,* without even a word said.

American spiritual teacher Ram Dass has spent many hours sitting with dying people and their families. He would often just sit for an hour or two, not saying anything at all. But the quality of his strongly compassionate presence (no doubt felt through mirror neurons, morphic resonance, and who knows what else) was palpable. At the end of his time with the dying and their loved ones, they would often thank him profusely and go on about how much he'd helped them. Since he'd just been sitting there, "doing" nothing, he was a bit bemused. But he kept on with this practice, and it kept helping people. Again, the key difference is that true Compassion joins us with another; Pity subtly separates us. Deep connection with another probably won't heal the dying, but it certainly can help us in almost any circumstance.

Sympathetic Joy: Near and Far Enemies

Last but not least is Sympathetic Joy. The Far Enemy, naturally enough, is Jealousy, competitiveness. As a matter of fact, when we feel jealous or competitive with another, the Buddha instructed us to cultivate Sympathetic Joy as the antidote.

Let's talk for a minute about the Far Enemy before moving on to the Near Enemy, because even though the Far Enemy is easier to spot, it can be awfully hard to work through. In that case we're going to be throwing someone out of our heart, thereby making Sympathetic Joy less than Boundless. Instead, our own heart shrinks.

Have you ever felt less than Sympathetic Joy when someone else just bought a nice car and you couldn't? Or when someone else just found a wonderful life partner while you were still unhappily single? Perhaps you have trouble feeling a whole lot of joy for them—or maybe any

Namchak weekend retreat

joy at all—because, let's face it, you don't get to have that same thing. But does their having it keep you from having it? Will your refusing to be happy for them help you to get that car or sweetie? Even if you can't celebrate those things for yourself, how will it hurt anything to celebrate it for them? Heck, at least you get to celebrate it for *someone*. Lots of people who are frustrated at not finding a sweetie get all sappily happy at romantic movies. If we can be happy for some imaginary people getting such things in movies without resenting them for it, why not in real life?

How about a case where someone you were competing with beat you out for first place? Of course it's all the more challenging to be happy for them. I wouldn't try this one right away. But someday you might challenge yourself with this one. You could again ask yourself, "Now that I already lost first place, how will it help me to resent the person who won it?" Just from a purely selfish point of view, resenting them won't get you first place after all. Again, given that you already didn't win, you could ask yourself, "How will it hurt anything to celebrate for the winner?" Again, at least that way you get to celebrate for *someone*, instead of just feeling crummy.

The Near Enemy is Hypocrisy—feigned appreciation of the person who's having good fortune. I hardly need to explain the difference between feigned Sympathetic Joy and the real thing. The difficulty here is in honestly admitting to faking it. Perhaps we *act* happy for the other person just to make ourselves feel or look like a good person—a good sport. But even if we aren't secretly jealous—the Far Enemy—we might, for example, be secretly passing judgment on their good fortune not being important or their not being worthy of it.

One conversation with my father, many years ago, illustrates this Near Enemy. I told him that I'd been accepted for a two-month apprenticeship program at an excellent acupressure clinic in California. They'd

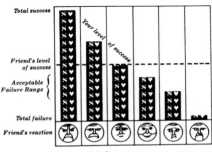

FIG. XX: FRIEND'S REACTIONS TO YOUR SUCCESS

Dan Greenburg, *How to Make Yourself Miserable*

never offered such an apprenticeship before, but they liked the idea and were willing to design one for me. I was thrilled! My father smiled faintly: "That's nice, honey." He said the right words, but rather than feeling that my joy was shared, I felt a pinprick in my balloon of excitement. Poof. Though he was smiling and saying nice words, his response served to separate us, not to join us in loving connection.

I knew my father didn't believe in any sort of alternative medicine. But that wasn't the point. I wasn't asking for him to share my opinion on the merits of acupressure; I wanted him to share my joy in receiving an honor and an opportunity that delighted me.*

How do we feel true Sympathetic Joy for someone when we're judging what they're happy about, don't like them, or feel competitive with them? It always helps me to remember that the person experiencing joy—even if it's not for reasons that would make me at all joyful—is wandering around in Samsara, just as confused as I am. They want to be happy as much as I do. They want to avoid suffering just as much too. If they've found a moment of joy in this bed of thorns, why not be happy for them? It doesn't hurt me one bit to feel that joy. In fact, it feels better than wishing they were miserable, or one-down. It feels better *to me*. In fact, whenever I tune in to the underlying we-ness of our humanity, our sentient beingness, I feel a relaxing in my heart. I breathe easier—no doubt because I've just fallen into right relationship with that person. In this small way, I've come closer to the way things truly are, closer to home.

I've found that by tuning in to our common ground, I can practice any of the Four Boundless Qualities even with people I dislike the most, even with people who have spent years waging campaigns against me. But remember, these challenges are not for our first forays into these practices. Just as we push the envelope gradually when we do hamstring stretches, we push the envelope gently but consistently with these practices.

Paradoxically, it's this gentle, gradual approach that yields the fastest results. If I do gentle hamstring stretches twice a day, every day for

---

* He was so set against any medical treatment that wasn't part of old-school Western medicine that many years later, when he was diagnosed with Parkinson's disease, he refused any of the new treatments and went only with the most conventional ones, even though they'd been proven by thousands not to work.

a short time, in a matter of weeks I can touch my palms to the floor. If I only do them once a week, I make no progress. It's been shown in scientific studies that after a few weeks of daily practice, people's capacity for loving connection, in various forms, improves dramatically. People's actions during the day change too. Stephen Post and Jill Neimark's book *Why Good Things Happen to Good People* offers discussion and examples of this principle.

As you continue to practice, you'll no doubt notice a difference for, and in, yourself. Others on the outside will notice it, but you'll probably notice even more difference on the inside. After training in these four ways of feeling more connected, less alone, how could you not help but feel that way, ongoing? And remember, there's no rule that says you have to stop when you get off the cushion. Just as with stretching hamstrings, you can speed up these changes by using these four methods whenever you think of it, during the course of daily life.

APPLIED BUDDHISM—*Sangha*
Stretching the stretching-the-hamstring metaphor till it's about ready to snap: a gymnast needs to do more than stretching their hamstrings to win a gold medal. They'll need to learn specific skills, practice them, then perform them in the actual Big Moment. So how do you *apply* your burgeoning capacity for connection with other people? At work, with your family, in your weekly study groups, or with the irascible lady in the checkout line? *These* are the Big Moment events in our lives.

For example, let's say you've been practicing Loving Kindness beautifully on your cushion for a month. It's your turn to lead the weekly study group, and the lady who's always talking is hogging the air time again. Meanwhile, there's a guy who never says a word. Tonight he's as silent as ever. You try to encourage him by gently asking him a question. He answers, "Yep." That's it. Then the chatty lady swoops in to fill the momentary vacuum. Nature abhors a vacuum, and so does she. Are you feeling that Loving Kindness now? What do you do? What do you say? Even if you do manage your own feelings, how do you work with everybody?

This is where many groups lose their chance to become real, satisfying communities, with deep, heartfelt connection. I'm talking about this because, remember, the Four Boundless Qualities are all about deep, heartfelt connection. You really want this for your group, but it looks like all of you—yourself included—might just want to give up and stay home.

There are real, practical skills for navigating this and other rocks in the water—even disagreement, power struggles, all the static that emerges when humans with their Afflictive Emotions (a.k.a. Three Poisons) get together in a group. We offer some simple guidance for you on our website, to get you started. But if you really want satisfying connection, that has to happen, well, in connection.

So we decided to offer live trainings—both in person and online—in what we're calling "Waking Up in Community." I think of it as "Applied Buddhism." Buddha means "one who's awake" and our efforts to wake up don't begin and end on the cushion. We want to take these principles off the cushion and *apply* them in our live interactions with fellow human beings. Imagine if you could do that in cahoots with other people who are co-conspiring to do the same thing! I mentioned in the last book that the Buddha spoke of Three Jewels—Buddha, Dharma, and Sangha. This last bit about Applied Buddhism/ Waking Up in Community is in the Sangha department. As I've mentioned before, if we go on a journey we want three things: a guide who's successfully reached the goal, the map that got them there, and fellow journeyers trying to go in the same direction. The Buddha is the guide, the Dharma is his map, and the Sangha is a community of fellow journeyers with a similar goal in mind.

> Imagine if you could do that in cahoots with other people who are co-conspiring to do the same thing!

Something the Buddha might not have spelled out clearly (but I will) is that the Sangha—your little Learning Circle—is a wonderful training ground between your inner work on the cushion and manifesting those capacities out in the wide world. Please check our website for a lively training that will already bring you satisfying connection, right there. And if you practice what you learn—bring your whole group!—you can have satisfying community in your life. If you don't have a group, you might find a person or two at the training to connect with afterward. Or contact us (info@Namchak.org) for names of people who might be in your area or available online. If you find fellow co-conspirators, we can send you a Toolkit for ideas and tips on how to start and continue. We feel this person-to-person aspect is so important that we offer a progression of Applied Buddhism training—a whole strand—that we weave into our approach, all the way through. We call it the Sangha strand. Maybe you're already part of a group where you can practice these things together. Maybe you don't feel that a Learning Circle is right for you. Still, you might try some arena for applying all this. Then fellow journeyers can support your practice, and it will continue to grow and be refreshed.

WE ALL PROJECT LIKE CRAZY. AND WE ALL JUST WANT TO BE SEEN

When I was in my twenties I noticed something odd. When I was with one group of people—conservatives—they saw me as The Hippie. But when I actually was around more hippie-ish folks, I was seen as The Conservative. "What gives?" I thought. "I'm the same person the whole time!" I noticed something else weird. When I was with the conservatives who thought I was a hippie flake, I found myself being swept along by the undertow of their opinion, and falling into more hippie-like behavior. And with the hippies I seemed to become more stick-in-the-mud conventional.

Again, what gives? I wanted so much for *everyone* just to see *me*. This phenomenon—being mistakenly and reductively typecast—wasn't happening just with random groups of people out there; it was happening with my husband, with all my family members, really. What a painful and lonely feeling. A few years later, when I studied the work of Carl Jung, I found he had some very helpful things to say.

Once we have our basic food/clothing/shelter needs met, one thing we human beings most desire is to be seen. Truly seen. Yet we humans constantly project on each other: we project assumptions, expectations, stereotypes, attributes, simplifications, unrealistic positives and negatives. You probably agree with my first statement, but maybe not the second one. But since projection is an unconscious process, of course we're the last to be conscious of our own unconscious. There's a bumper sticker for you!

What is projection, anyway? How does it work? Carl Jung popularized this concept. He understood that we all have some version of all characteristics and characters floating around inside, somewhere. As our personalities form, we take some of those and consciously identify with them: *I'm* a savior/warrior (activists, are you listening?), *I'm* the class clown, *I'm* a geek, bad boy, and on and on. I'm the Nurturing Father type, I'm the Dependable One, and on and on. But what about all of the other qualities and characters that we aren't claiming with our conscious mind?

They're underground—in the basement. The ones we really don't want to claim, we do our best to keep in the dank darkness of that basement. What happens with all of those, while the ones we've set out in the sunshine are developing nicely? Instead of getting a chance to develop and mature, they kind of fester. They get frustrated and funky. And trust me, they don't stay obediently in the basement forever.

With both the positive and negative ones, for one reason or another we aren't able to see them in ourselves. So they're, by definition, residing in our unconscious.

In my days as a psychotherapist, I had all kinds of characteristics and characters projected onto me. Wise Woman. Best Friend and Confidante. You can be sure I got people's mothers projected onto me: the Mother They Wished They'd Had—or, if they got disappointed, then I was their Bad Mother. (I suspect their actual, 3–D mother wasn't really that Bad.)

And in my everyday life, I've also had all kinds of things projected onto me. Wallflower, uppity woman (yes, somebody actually called me that), spiritual person, practical person, artsy type, Jew and therefore good with money (yikes!), and on and on. I've noticed that when someone makes a strong projection on me, no matter what I do, I just seem to confirm what they're already projecting. Of course I'm uncomfortable with negative projections, but actually, I'm uncomfortable with positive ones too. Because neither, whether derogatory or supposedly flattering, are the real me (or at least what I believe is the real me!). Over time, I've come to realize that everybody's projecting on me all the time. People I don't know very well, my closest friends, my family members, co-workers, everybody. And through it all, *I just want to be seen.*

Have you ever noticed something like that happening to you? If you're a woman, maybe it seems like people think you're not as smart or capable as you actually are. If you're a man, maybe someone thinks you're more aggressive than you actually are. Or that you're the reverse—a doormat—when you're really not. Or perhaps someone projects onto you more patience than you can usually sustain, or more expertise in a particular area than you actually possess. Maybe you've had different—even opposite—projections from different people.

By now I'm thinking of that famous saying, "Everyone's crazy but thee and me. And sometimes I wonder about thee!" We're thinking it's everyone else who's projecting like mad. Um, how about you and me?

Yuck. Is there a way out of this?

Yes. Let's look at one example from the West, and one from the East. Let's start with a look at how some in the West work with projection. As I mentioned, Carl Jung, who popularized this idea of projection in the West, believed that we have all possible characters inside of us, even though we identify with only a few. Again, we've relegated all the others to the basement. He used dream interpretation and something called active imagination to try to coax them into our conscious mind.

I was lucky enough to go to a Jungian analyst who, borrowing from Fritz Perls's Gestalt work, had me sit in another chair and *become* some disowned part of myself. I then went back and forth between the two chairs, having a conversation. I found this approach extremely clarifying and helpful, and immediately tried it out with a client with a terrible procrastination problem. I had her go back and forth between two chairs: one was like her older sister, whom she saw as overbearing, and the other was like her more childish self. The two had a rousing debate over what she should do with her weekend—party or study. Each of them passionately insisted they had her best interests at heart. They were both right.

Then I had her sit in the middle and be the peacemaker. She got them to forge a deal to alternate between partying and studying. All of this was a revelation to her. She had identified only with the fun-loving gal. Then in desperate moments, her other side would come out of the basement and be a slave driver. In this conversation, she found that she could make a clear plan to have a balanced, happy weekend that didn't jeopardize either her happiness or her grade point average. And it expanded her identity, her sense of herself. Her view of her older sister changed too. I bet her sister was relieved.

There are other, very effective ways to work with projection of our various inner characters, and we don't even have to pay a therapist. What if we could meet with a few people who want to work together on this, and made an agreement? It would go something like this: We admit that we're all projecting on each other all the time, and we're each the last to know we're doing it. Usually the projec*tee* knows way sooner than the projec*tor*. So let's make a deal: If you gently tell me what you're perceiving, hopefully with specific examples because I'll probably be clueless, I'll do the same for you.

We both give each other permission to do this. We both learn how to do this with skill and kindness. Note that this approach works for both the projector and the projectee—the projector can let us know what they're seeing in us; the projectee can share what they think the projector might be inaccurately (or incompletely, and certainly unintentionally) projecting onto them. And vice versa.

Imagine if we all did that simple thing. We'd get better and better at knowing what's going on with our disowned parts—the good and bad ones—and get much better at taking back our projections. We might have trouble doing this if we don't do some work inside with those disowned parts, getting to know them and refining them after all those years in the basement.

While Carl Jung did get at the internal work to some extent, I found the Tibetan Buddhist practices far more efficient and profound at doing it. The array of Tibetan practices offer myriad tools that help us to bring all the characters out of the basement, in their fullest, most highly developed forms, and to own them. There are the One Hundred Peaceful and Wrathful Deities, as well as practices involving various enlightened masters. Each is an image of an archetype—a facet or principle of reality. And being principles of reality, they're all everywhere, including in each of us.

An archetype is like one of those snowflake stencils many of us created as kids by making little cuts in a piece of paper. You spray paint through it and when you take it away, voila—a snowflake you can make again and again. Once you use the stencil, you just see the painted snowflake. Jungians like to use the metaphor of a magnet hidden under a piece of paper that has iron filings on it. As you move the hidden magnet, it draws the filings into different shapes. We see only the shapes of the filings, not the magnet.

Let's take the Great Mother archetype, a principle of reality that's everywhere, including inside of us. In Tibetan practice context, both men and women practice Green Tara as what Jung called an "archetypal image." They invoke that principle from outside and evoke it

Green Tara: Tibetan image of the Great Mother archetype

from the inside. Since we have trouble relating to the pure unseen principle/archetype, we use image (a beautiful green lady), archetypal sound (mantra), and even smell (incense).

The classic progression is that we consciously project Tara out from our hearts, where Tibetan Buddhists believe our mind mainly resides. We project her above us, seeing her clearly in our mind's eye. We all tend to think out internal conversations and dramas with people. But in this case, the setup for our connection with Green Tara is perfectly designed to give us a much more profound, powerful, and enlightened experience than, say, imagining calling our earthly mom on the phone. Though our mom is just a human being, with faults and foibles, Green Tara is the image that naturally evokes the perfect facet of enlightened mind that is the essence of the mother principle.

Here we do this progression: inviting her, welcoming her, asking her to sit, offering her water and flowers, and so on. Then we say the mantra associated with her: *Om tarey tuttarey turey soha.*

Often we then imagine her descending into us, dissolving into us, becoming indistinguishable from us. We emerge as Tara ourselves. We continue to see ourselves as Tara, in our mind's eye, say and hear the mantra, and so on, grounding ourselves ever more strongly in the owning of that pure archetype.

Now let's look at a negative character scenario. Let's take Fred, for an imaginary example. He thinks of himself as a Mr. Nice Guy. This means that when people want to walk all over him, he doesn't have the wherewithal, in his conscious array of characters, to assert himself. His Tough Guy or Warrior is in the basement. It's been lurking there all his life, and isn't very presentable as a result. Whenever Fred gets cornered, he suddenly bites the person's head off . . . then regrets it later, and may not even get what he needs. Sociologist and life coach Martha Beck refers to this as an "exploding doormat."

Fred might do well to practice Hayagriva, a fierce, enlightened being of a class known as protectors. They can act with great ferocity, but always with wisdom and compassion. If he were to inhabit Hayagriva the way we talked of inhabiting/owning Tara, he would find his way to the *pure essence* of that murky, funky character who popped out when he exploded. Once he'd spent time owning and in*habit*ing Hayagriva, Fred is much more likely to skillfully, kindly, and firmly ward off people walking all over him.

Whether it's a peaceful one like Tara or a more wrathful one like Hayagriva, we fully *own* the archetype. It has gone from something we can't see or feel, to a pure presence that we fully identify with. Over time, as we get used to owning that presence consciously, we have little need to project it onto someone else. And in owning this purer form, we can often bring forth those qualities in everyday life. They're much more at our fingertips.

In Tibetan Buddhist deity practice, the goal is to take us from our usual banal, confused state to *dak-nang*, or pure vision—seeing things as they really are. Imagine if everyone did such well-honed practices, on a lot of different deities. I believe we would then be able to take the various characters out of our basements, develop them, and "play" them in various moments in life. Playing with a full deck, you might say!

And this serves the essential intent of the Buddha: that we use practices to wake ourselves from the dream/trance that we find ourselves in. (Remember, "buddha" means "one who is awake.") In truth, reality is a vast, perfect ocean, which loves to create ever-changing waves and play with them. This ocean is bursting, overflowing with love and joy. But most of us waves don't see it that way. We don't realize that we're not just a wave, but made of ocean. *We are* all *wave and ocean.*

Imagine if we all used both the Tibetan methods AND the Western methods. We wouldn't have the urge to project onto each other quite as much, and we would have methods for catching ourselves and each other in the act. When it inevitably happens, we'd have skills that bring us closer together in camaraderie rather than causing us to build walls of protection and projection against each other.

That's what we encourage people to do in our Namchak Learning Circles. We offer a weekend training in which we learn not only about projections, but also about how to work compassionately and skillfully to talk about them with each other. As you can imagine, that last part is important!

On a societal level, imagine if a critical mass of people became fluent in these skills and capacities. The whole culture would be affected. There would be less of a need to call some other demographic stupid, lazy, conniving, and on and on. How different this world would be. I believe this is not just "pie in the sky" but something we all must do, to solve the problems that now threaten our happiness and our very existence.

Hayagriva: image of the Tibetan enlightened, fierce protector archetype

We could progress from the swarm of projections—both societal and personal, which cause such pain—to really seeing each other. Then we could all relax our defenses—because those projections feel terrible—and we could work together to solve the dire problems we're all actually facing. And beyond even that, we'd find that human relations can be much simpler than we thought! They can be deeply connected, warm, and delicious. And we can be seen.

PLAY WITH IT—YOU'RE IN CHARGE!

Now that you've gotten a handshake introduction to the Four Boundless Qualities, you're ready to begin using them to expand your capacity to connect with your fellow sentient beings in a meaningful, satisfying way. In addition to your practice on the cushion, doing a workout for your heart (no, not cardio!), also take the time to look once in awhile to see if your increasing capacity is also showing up in everyday life.

When should you do which Boundless Quality? It's up to you! When you've been doing one for a while and you feel it's not so fresh anymore, switch to another.

FOLDING THE FOUR BOUNDLESS QUALITIES INTO THE ROUND ROBIN

As we go along, I'm sure you've noticed that the practices you've already learned get folded into the next ones. Now we've been folding the Four Boundless Qualities into your Round Robin daily practice. For example, in place of the Tonglen you practiced yesterday, you might practice Sympathetic Joy in that part of the Round Robin today. In fact, Rinpoche recommends that if you've been doing a whole lot of Tonglen and are feeling a bit down, Sympathetic Joy brings you up, making a nice balance. Mary Oliver managed to hold those two in her heart at once, in a moving poem she wrote. When I read it, I recalled the soaring awe I feel every fall, as the geese fly over my head, sounding their thrilling call . . . yet the poem also touched me with compassion so that I wept.

At the Pond
BY MARY OLIVER

One summer
    I went every morning
        to the edge of a pond where
            a huddle of just hatched geese

would paddle to me
    and clamber
        up the marshy slope
            and over my body,

peeping and staring—
    such sweetness every day
        which the grown ones watched,
            for whatever reason,

serenely.
    Not there, however, but here
        is where the story begins.
            Nature has many mysteries,

some of them severe.
    Five of the young geese grew
        heavy of chest and
            bold of wing

while the sixth waited and waited
    in its gauze-feathers, its body
        that would not grow.
            And then it was fall.

And this is what I think
    everything is all about:
        the way
            I was glad

for those five and two
    that flew away,
        and the way I hold in my heart the wingless one
            that had to stay.

If you've been gradually expanding from the five minutes of Tonglen practice, good! I'm sure your capacity for compassion has grown hugely (immeasurably?). If you feel like it, you could do ten minutes of Tonglen followed by five minutes of Sympathetic Joy. Or perhaps today you feel like practicing ten minutes straight—of Loving Kindness, for example. Eventually you could do fifteen. Again, this is something that feels good but is completely legal, moral, and non-fattening!* As I mentioned in Book 1, despite feeling resistance to sitting down to practice, I get up feeling better—more deeply satisfied and happy—than what any fifteen minutes (maybe even longer!) of an official vacation could provide.

Recently, I was visiting a friend and came down with a dreadful cold. I was complaining to her that (because I was visiting her) I didn't feel obligated to do work, but now I was too sick to do practice. She said, "Don't feel like you have to be productive, just relax—you're sick." I tried to explain to her that practicing is a beautiful, profound experience and I come out of it feeling lovely. She doesn't do daily practice so didn't quite get it.

Remember, by stepping the concentric rings out, in all the practices, you're practicing Equanimity—equally strong connection with *all*—when you're practicing any of the other three. But if you want to focus just on Boundless Equanimity, getting down to that basic loving connection to all beings, then of course you can do that in the Four Boundless Qualities part of the Round Robin too. Remember, Rinpoche advises us that Equanimity takes a primary place, because without it, none of the others will be "Boundless."

Now that you're ready to go, here's a sample daily practice page. You have a lot to play with now.

Experiment. Play! Savor. Settle in.

---

* Frank Rand, popularized by Alexander Woollcott on his radio show in 1933. The full quote (though there are variations, since it wasn't originally in written form) goes something like this: " . . . it seems as if anything I like is either illegal, immoral, or fattening." It's been often and fondly quoted ever since.

As with the first volume and with the individual Boundless Quality Round Robin practices, I've included a Weekly Progression Guideline card in an envelope in the back of this book too, so you can have it in front of you on your practice table. All of this is to help you get started, and to support you in following through. The Weekly Progression is just a suggestion. You can use it to remind you of any practice you might have been forgetting lately, for example. Now you're ready to go for months!

You might not want to miss various supports out there. I don't know about all the groups around, but I recommend a few in this book and in Book 2. Of course, we have some too. There are many benefits to live instruction, webinars, recordings, weekend retreats, and weekly meetings with your group. Why practice in a total vacuum? Hearing from more experienced people who have chewed on these concepts for years is great input that a book alone—even one as well-intentioned as this one!—just can't give you. And chewing together with fellow students, on life's challenges and how these might help, is so alive and satisfying!

As for webinars and live instruction, many Jewish women (including this one) like to tell this joke:

> *"Why did we wander for forty years in the desert?"*
> *"Because the guys wouldn't ask for directions."*

My advice: don't wander alone for forty years.

Weekly Progression Guideline

I want to be clear: *this is only a guideline,* for those days when you don't notice something happening *for you in the moment,* or you can't decide which practice(s) to do. If some sound, feeling, or thought is up for you, *it's best to go with that.* If it's Wednesday and the Guideline lists focusing on form but there's a lot of noise, switch to sound instead. If something big has happened and you have a strong emotion about it, use that emotion as your support. In other words, *work with what's happening,* and use it as your support. Remember that Tibetan Buddhism meets us as, and where, we are—so if something is particularly intense for you where you are, go with that.

MONDAY
- **THEME FOR SHAMATA:** Breath
- **THEME FOR FOUR BOUNDLESS QUALITIES:** Equanimity

TUESDAY
- **THEME FOR SHAMATA:** Form (image on card)
- **THEME FOR FOUR BOUNDLESS QUALITIES:** Loving Kindness

WEDNESDAY
- **THEME FOR SHAMATA:** Form
- **THEME FOR FOUR BOUNDLESS QUALITIES:** Compassion (Tonglen)

THURSDAY
- **THEME FOR SHAMATA:** Sensation or Sound
- **THEME FOR FOUR BOUNDLESS QUALITIES:** Equanimity

FRIDAY
- **THEME FOR SHAMATA:** Thoughts or Emotions (pick one)
- **THEME FOR FOUR BOUNDLESS QUALITIES:** Sympathetic Joy

SATURDAY
- **THEME FOR SHAMATA:** Breath
- **THEME FOR FOUR BOUNDLESS QUALITIES:** Tonglen

SUNDAY
- **THEME FOR SHAMATA:** Form
- **THEME FOR FOUR BOUNDLESS QUALITIES:** Compassion alternated with Sympathetic Joy

Namchak Retreat Ranch

THE SIX PARAMITAS

The six *Paramitas*, or Transcendent Perfections, that we'll need on the path are Generosity, Discipline, Forbearance, Joyful Effort, Concentration, and Wisdom. In Buddhism, many concepts come in pairs, as you've seen. Another pair is wisdom and skillful means. The first five of the Paramitas are all facets of skillful means. Transcendent wisdom, is, well, wisdom. Here, then, is a bit more of an explanation of these qualities that will serve you well. If you're particularly low on one, you may want to focus on boosting it. They're worth boosting because you need them all in good measure, to succeed on this path—well, when you think about it, in life.

Transcendent Generosity

One king was downright pitiful in the generosity department. When the master he was studying with told him of the importance of practicing generosity, he cried, "But I have no capacity for that at all! How can I practice it?" The master was very wise and knew what we've been talking about here: that if we force ourselves to practice in a way far beyond our capacity, we'll snap back like a rubber band to our old ways of acting. Too much generosity and we resent it, which ruins the karmic benefit and will probably be followed by a snapping back to selfish behavior. If we don't challenge ourselves *some*, though, we won't make any progress. So the master asked the king to pick up a nearby orange. "Do you have enough generosity that you can *give* that orange to your left hand?" "Yes!" cried the delighted king. He actually hesitated. Even giving to his own left hand was a bit of a stretch. "Good," intoned the master. "Begin with doing that back and forth until you're completely comfortable with it, and expand from there."

The king enthusiastically practiced this many times until he was ready to stretch a bit more. The master gave him slightly bigger and bigger challenges to his generosity, which he also enthusiastically practiced many times a day. After a time, the king gave vast amounts of his wealth and possessions to his subjects. His kingdom flourished and he became known as a master of generosity.

Try working with yourself in that way, on whatever your weakest points are.

Under the generosity category, there are the sub-categories of: 1) material giving, which is obvious; 2) giving the Dharma, which helps people's minds, therefore their whole experience, karma, etc. (can you tell that that's a personal favorite of mine?); and 3) protection from fears, the most virtuous example of which is saving a life.

Transcendent Discipline

Some people translate this as "Ethics" or "Ethical Discipline." Obviously, if we don't have enough discipline, we won't practice any of the other methods, either during or out of sessions. Without this one, it's a non-starter. *With* this one, you're able to do your sessions and apply the methods. Outside of sessions, you're able to steer your behavior toward virtuous acts and away from non-virtuous ones . . . which you'll really want to do, not just out of compassion for those around you, but even for your own sake. As we know, this is essential for cleaning your kar-mic windshield. Of course a clean windshield, in turn, helps you apply the mind-training methods during your sessions. Improvement in *that*, in turn, helps you to improve your actions *in between* sessions. And so on. This positive cycle is what we want to have happen—inner work and outer behavior helping each other along. This will speed up your progress exponentially. Again, do as the master advised the selfish king: start where you ARE, always gently stretching the rubber band of your capacity, so that it doesn't snap back, but gradually grows. Anyone who's tried to diet knows about the rubber band.

Bison at the Namchak Retreat Ranch

Transcendent Forbearance

This one is seen as the antidote for anger. Though it's commonly translated as "patience," I actually agree with one translator who uses "forbearance" instead. *Patience* implies waiting—sometimes waiting for things to change, or waiting until it's time for you to do what you have in mind, even if what you have in mind may be ignoble or petty. In other words, you could *patiently* wait until it's time to exact your revenge on someone who's wronged you. *Forbearance*, though, suggests letting go of your impulse to react to provocation; it's a "yes, but" perspective. For example, "Yes, I could see why this might make someone angry, but I'm working on responding with wisdom and compassion." Or, "Yes, this practice is hard and sometimes tedious and painful, but I'm not going to complain and I'm certainly not going to give up." Or, "This is a hard and scary truth to face, but I'm not going to turn away from truth."

There are three aspects to this Transcendent quality: 1) forbearance when wronged; 2) forbearing the hardships of Dharma practice; 3) fearless forbearance when looking profound truth—emptiness—in the face.

We've discussed how essential it is to avoid more splatters on our karmic windshield if we want to reach liberation. There is no worse way to lose virtuous karma (merit) and gain lots of negative karma than by losing our temper. In *The Way of the Bodhisattva*, it says:

All the good works gathered in a thousand ages,
Such as deeds of generosity.
And offerings to the Blissful Ones—
A single flash of anger shatters them.

On the other hand, when somebody harms us, if we don't get angry but instead accept their anger toward us as a way for us to pay off some of our karmic debt, we can turn the experience into a huge benefit for ourselves. Now we need more hands: on the one hand, that karma is now exhausted, so we can feel pleased about that. On the other, we've just taken the opportunity to practice Forbearance, which adds to our arsenal for pursuing an upward spiral. If we don't practice Forbearance at those times, *when better?* And rather than feeling reciprocal anger at that person, we can feel gratitude for what they gave us:

"How would you feel if the mouse did that to you?"

opportunities not only to discharge karma but also to practice a virtue. And the only way to practice Forbearance is to be in a circumstance that would otherwise spark our anger, frustration, or fear.

You might recall Rinpoche's time in prison as an extreme example of this one. At first, as a thirteen-year-old boy ripped from his family and made by his conquerors to do hard labor, he was extremely resentful. Under the tutelage of one of the greatest "hidden lamas" of the twentieth century, Tulku Orgyen Chemchok, Rinpoche came to see that he was paying off lots of bad karma while getting the chance to practice Transcendent Forbearance. He fully took the opportunity. Not only did it change his karmic balance sheet, it transformed his experience in prison to a happy one! He could even feel compassion for the guards, who were busily sowing the seeds of unimaginable suffering for themselves.

We can use this perspective as a yardstick to measure our progress too. If we continue to be as sensitive as ever to criticism and negative gossip about ourselves, we need to admit our practice isn't doing us much good. We're simply not making progress on this journey. On the other hand, despite our distractions in meditation and all the rest, if we find we're much more at ease with such things, we have real "proof in the pudding" that we've made progress.

HELPFUL HINTS

One metaphor that really helps me to Forbearance when I've been wronged is to see all of us sentient beings—me too—writhing around in a mud pit. We're slipping and sliding around with almost no control. It's crowded, and I accidentally step on somebody's shoulder. "OW!" they cry. Later I fall down and somebody kicks my ear. OW! What's the point in getting mad at somebody who's got no more control than I do?

In *A Guide to the Bodhisattva Way of Life*, the early Indian Buddhist master Shantideva gives another metaphor. If someone hits you with a stick, do you get mad at the stick? What's the point? The stick has no control. How about the hand wielding the stick? Well, neither does the person, who's driven by anger and is powerless to stop themselves. Rinpoche brought this perspective to his prison experience.

Yet another metaphor I like is from *Gates to Buddhist Practice*, by Chagdud Tulku.* He sees a person acting in anger like someone jumping into a raging river. It's certain to bring disaster. If we jump into the torrent after them, we're subjecting ourselves to the same fate. That's what happens when we meet anger with anger.

On to the next form of Transcendent Forbearance: forbearing the hardships of the Dharma can be as simple as waking up early enough to practice, even though we're really tired. That's a big one, actually, isn't it?! As with all the Paramitas, we can get used to this one until after a time it becomes easy. We wonder why we found it so painful before. After all, when we travel we can get used to a new time zone, which is at least a whole hour different.

For an extreme example, we can bring Milarepa to mind. He lived with various unbearable hardships for years, pursuing enlightenment. When I consider him, I think, "Who am I, to complain that I'm sleepy this morning?" (Okay, I also take a cup of tea along to my practice place.)

Forbearing Facing Into Reality may not be so obvious to some. I've described reality as being this blissful state. But for now, we don't experience it that way: we're that single wave, who secretly knows (despite

---

*   *Gates to Buddhist Practice: Essential Teachings of a Tibetan Master* by Chagdud Tulku © Padma Publishing 1993, © Revised Edition 2001. Published by Padma Publishing. California.

its best attempts to ignore the fact) they're going to experience the fate of all waves. It will take a while before we truly feel that we're the ocean. At this point it's not easy for us to truly face the fact that there's no "I," no substantial body, nothing to hang onto—it's actually quite terrifying. We don't walk around in big boots like that one scientist did, fearing his insubstantial body would fall through the floor. But we have other ways of reassuring ourselves that we're "real" (in the solid, constant form that we think we are). How many of us aren't afraid of dying? Isn't dying the ultimate version of Facing Into Reality? Again, we have to approach that one gradually . . . yet steadily. Of course, we'd like to be comfortable with this one before we have to die and experience it full force.

Transcendent Joyful Effort

You've probably noticed by now that I really focus on the "joyful" part of the effort because then I'll be more likely to *make* the effort! If we expect to feel good as a result of our efforts, it makes those efforts feel like part of the whole happy experience.

When I was growing up, I remember noticing that the best part of Passover was working in the kitchen with my mother and sister, preparing all the yummy foods for the feast, setting the table just so, and dressing up. In the same spirit, I've made a beautiful place for my practice, with everything arranged just so, having gathered this or that little treasure over the years. I put on my prayer shawl and settle into a beautiful, profound experience (well, in between distractions). As I've said, the mind works largely through association. Over time, I've had many profound, beautiful, and powerful experiences in that place, doing those practices. All of this contributes to the "joyful" part of the effort. So I suggest you, too, keep your eye toward the joyful part of the effort, always remembering that one joyful part is the true happiness that comes from the *fruits* of that effort. The other truly can be the journey. After all, the practice isn't the enlightenment, but we can enjoy the practice.

As for the "Effort" part, you can see why this one is on the list of necessary qualities on the path. Without it, we simply have another non-starter. But isn't that true with anything worthwhile? The great master Jigmey Lingpa likened the pursuit of the Dharma without Joyful Effort to a boat with no oars. Dead in the water. Or helplessly carried around by the water.

Following spread: The Stupa Garden at Namchak Retreat Ranch

Transcendent Concentration

Clearly we can't get anywhere using any of the mind-training methods without this one either; yet we start the path with precious little of it. We've talked about this catch-22, and again, the answer is gentle perseverance—Joyful Effort, not to mention Forbearance! Now we have brain studies to show that we can make huge changes in our brains, like water on stones, over time. What surprised me about those studies was that measurable change started within weeks. If we cultivate concentration more and more, as our capacity grows, then we can make progress with all of our other goals.

It's fairly obvious that if we want to concentrate well, we have to eliminate (or at least firmly minimize) distractions. On the face of it, a distraction could mean answering the phone while meditating, or having a TV going in your meditation area. Less obvious are the distractions of your life. As you're pursuing the things and people you want and trying to eliminate those you don't want, you're providing another level of distraction. These fixations are at least as threatening to your concentration as the phone or TV. Notice the inner conversations and strategizing that continually push their way into your meditations. The more we realize the futility of hoping that the things of Samsara will bring us real, lasting happiness, the more we naturally turn away from those things—let go of them. Once again, we need to let go of all hope and fear, as much as we can. That in turn, allows us to pursue this path with less distraction. The resulting progress allows us to feel real satisfaction and happiness more and more. Again, the upward spiral of this path.

Transcendent Wisdom

In other sections of this book, in various ways, I've urged you to take in the words found here, as well as those from other teachers. Follow that by contemplating the meaning of the words, then actually do the practices.

I spoke of these three in Book 2: hear, contemplate, meditate. These as a whole will bring us Transcendent Wisdom. If we're missing any of those pieces, it will be difficult for us to gain much wisdom.

Of course, we need to begin the cycle with instruction. Why re-invent the wheel? If there is a qualified teacher who can transmit information that has successfully led people to liberation, why try to figure it out for yourself? But it's not enough to hear the words. Without asking questions, seeing how these concepts actually work in your mind and your life, you aren't digesting what you've taken in. Remember, the Buddha didn't think much of blind faith. He was a big proponent of a well-examined faith because then it can become the faith of knowing for yourself. So contemplation is the natural next part of the cycle.

The final step to the faith of knowing for yourself is what comes from our actual experience. The word for practice in Tibetan is *nyam-len*, which means "gain experience." For those who would like to learn strictly from experience, I would remind them that without instruction they can't use the mind-training tools properly and they won't gain the intended experience. So two more truths: we need expert instruction *and* we need to apply that instruction through ardent and sustained practice.

It really takes all three of these—hearing, contemplation, and meditation—to arrive at Transcendent Wisdom.

One practice that obviously helps us with Transcendent Wisdom is *Vipassana.* It's terribly important to all branches of Buddhism because of course we need to be able to see directly into the true nature of our minds, reality, and the relationship between them. I find that pursuit fascinating. It's also essential to apply Transcendent Wisdom to so many of the other qualities we're cultivating. For example, we've talked a bit about compassion without wisdom really being what Chögyam Trungpa Rinpoche calls 'idiot compassion.' So as with all of these Transcendent Perfections, we need a great deal of this one in order to benefit from the others . . . and the Dharma.

Section Two

VIPASSANA—SUBLIME INSIGHT

BIRD'S-EYE VIEW OF INSIGHT

Y ou might be wondering why on earth you'd need yet another practice. One big reason for me is that I *love* investigating how my mind works, how reality works, and the relationship between the two. In Vipassana, we get to really sink into a deep investigation of all that, with well-tested guidance from those who have really mastered that understanding. But there's another reason that takes a little explaining. Read on!

Before we go further, I just want to say that if you're reading this section, I hope it's because you've been doing the Round Robin with Shamata pretty much every day for at least six months. You have preferably gone to a retreat or two to jump-start your practice, and to learn more than my little written introduction can give you. Hopefully you've gotten live instruction from someone who is better at it than I am, such as Namchak Khen Rinpoche Ngawang Gelek.

My point is that you'll want to have your Shamata somewhat stabilized before starting this practice of Vipassana—Sublime Insight. Rinpoche says that Vipassana won't help much if your mind is still too wildly unstable. We're not looking for perfection, but if your mind isn't at least a little bit settled, Rinpoche likens it to a candle in a windy spot. In other words, it won't be strong enough for you to do the enlightening part with Vipassana. One standard that Tibetans often use is to see if the image they've been using as their Shamata support appears clearly in their mind's eye, even when they're not looking at the image. The other is that your mind doesn't feel like a waterfall when you're meditating, more like a slow river; better yet, a great, placid ocean. If that's the case for you, you're probably ready for Vipassana.

Even more than with Shamata, after reading this introduction to Vipassana you'll find the practice makes a whole lot more sense, and is benefiting you more if you've gone to live teachings. Best of all, if you get the chance, do at least a weekend practice retreat. We offer them occasionally, and Insight Meditation Society, Spirit Rock, Tergar, and the Goenka Group offer them all the time. Thousands of people have found them to be life changing.

By now you've probably seen how beautifully Shamata pairs with Tonglen or any of the Four Boundless Qualities. You've also seen how moving back and forth between them keeps your practice session fresh and alive. There's something else to be paired with Shamata—even more closely paired. In fact, you practice the two right in the same section of the Round Robin. Yes, Vipassana. They're designed to go together!

Back to that question: why do we need yet another technique, anyway? For the second answer to that, let's go directly to the teachings of the Buddha—a passage from *The Sutra of Definitive Commentary on the Enlightened Intent.* No, the title isn't longer than the teaching. One of the Buddha's students asks him a question about abiding and insight, and the Buddha replies. The student addresses the Buddha as "Bhagavan," indicating supreme, loving respect.

> *"O transcendent and accomplished conqueror, how many supports are there for calm abiding?"*
> *The Buddha replied, "Just one: an image that involves no conceptual thought."*
> *"O transcendent and accomplished conqueror, how many supports are there for profound insight?"*
> *The Buddha replied, "Just one: an image that involves conceptual thought."*

Are you confused? I sure was. Rinpoche quoted this in the Root Text of his recent book on Shamata, at the beginning of the last section, which is on Vipassana (Sublime Insight). When I read the quote, I couldn't imagine what this meant! I begged him to include a commentary in his book, from a recording of his live teachings on the subject, and he agreed. Now that his book is available, I highly recommend you get it. Until then, I'll do as I do throughout this whole trilogy: give you a handshake introduction as best I know how. Again, this brief introduction is meant only to give you a ramp-up to the fascinating and profound understandings that live teachings from an accomplished master can give you. We will offer Dharma teachings on various topics including Vipassana, and they are also available from other Dharma groups. Trust me, you won't really be able to get very far with Vipassana on the little bit that I'm giving you here. Here, then, is my best attempt at condensing Rinpoche's explanation, as I understood it from a transcript of his live teachings, and my notes at that time and several other times:

By "non-conceptual image" in Shamata, he meant that it's like an image in a mirror: just the plain, simple image, with no thought-commentary like "Ooh, this is pretty", or "I don't like that" and so on. Just the image. When we're resting our minds in Shamata, the Three Poisons are temporarily out of the, er, picture.

To understand the kind of benefit of sitting in this state, Rinpoche likens this to a field after a wildfire has roared over it, burning the grass to the ground. Let's say the field is crabgrass, a weed I've battled a lot in all my years of gardening, because it chokes out all the nutritious plants I'm trying to cultivate. Underneath the ground, the matted crabgrass roots are alive and well, even after the wildfire. After the next rainfall, the entire field is green with new crabgrass shoots. So in Shamata we can sit calmly, with a break in the usually constant flow of thoughts and emotions (well, more or less). But after a short time, the familiar emotions spring up again, at a moment's notice.

There was a lady behind me in a Shamata retreat, who kept making some kind of scratching noise. I couldn't figure out what that odd noise was, and I wove back and forth between resting in Shamata and being annoyed. "How *could* she? During a Shamata retreat, no less!" I thought. I did eventually come to accept it and simply be aware of it like any other noise: the birds chirping, the wind blowing, trees occasionally rustling, the lady mysteriously and annoyingly scratching.

When the retreat was over, we were allowed to speak, just before we left. I ended up talking to that lady. She turned out to be wise and kind, and grandmotherly, in a refined, intellectual sort of way. I liked her. I indulged my curiosity and asked her what (the heck) that scratching sound was. "I'm sorry," she said, "I'm a poet, and I couldn't help but try to capture some of the experience in little phrases." Later I bought a book of her poems and very much liked them. Since that time I've been irritated by thousands of things. They've helped my Shamata practice thousands of times.

Shamata is indeed an essential experience to have and to train in. But in this business of waking up, clearly we need something more. You've probably already noticed. Resting our minds on one thing for a bit is not really the same as awakening.

Back to the field of crabgrass that we'd hoped would be our garden. Clearly, picking the weeds out by the roots would be a more long-lasting solution. So how *do* we pluck those Afflictive/Neurotic/Poisonous Emotions out by the roots? This brings us to the second line in the quote, "an image of form together with conceptuality." In Vipassana we actually *use the concepts*, in order to realize that they have no inherent reality. We look with penetrating insight, right into the quintessence of that very thought/emotion/phenomenon.

This is the way to pull out the roots that later turn into full-blown dramas of the mind. And Samsara is nothing if not a full-blown drama of the mind. As we've seen in Shamata, we sign up for the dramas moment by moment, and then keep renewing our subscription. The moments string together into little dramas, the little dramas into bigger ones, the bigger ones giving birth to more little ones, until you've spun out a whole lifetime-drama. Then another. Then another.

Now maybe you see why you might want to get beneath the surface "weeds" and pull the roots out. Now you see the other very important reason to spend time with this practice.

As for the first answer—the adventure of investigating the mind and reality—scientists are great adventurers, on a lifelong journey of exploration, investigating how the universe works. The scientists at Mind And Life (with His Holiness the Dalai Lama) were intrigued to embark on the *inner* investigation of Vipassana, but as I'd mentioned before, they were wary of using the *observer's mind* as the investigative instrument. Instead of working with *objective* experience, they would have to use *subjective* experience. That's a huge no-no in Western science.

Not only that, but the item they would be investigating was often that mind, itself, making the whole enterprise potentially circular and solipsistic. (As songwriter Harold Rome asked, "Who's gonna investigate the man who investigates the man who investigates me?") But quantum physicists (and many others) will willingly admit that it's actually impossible to eliminate the observer as a factor in the experiments. The Buddha developed methods that would hone the observer's mind sufficiently to render it a worthy investigative tool. The scientists decided to give this unprecedented (in their experience) approach a try and did a ten-day Vipassana retreat.

In Book 2, I mentioned that psychiatrist Daniel Siegel writes a hysterical and inspiring rendition of his own experience at that retreat. Since he had never done retreat before, he started out going stir-crazy. In the middle of the retreat, his mind finally fell into a much more quiet state and he was able to perceive and experience reality utterly differently. It was as though he saw the trees—really saw them—for the first time. He tasted the food as he'd never tasted food before. His mind and heart were steady and open as they had never been before. He and the other scientists decided they wanted a steady diet of this training.

How about you?

Rinpoche put it yet another way. In both Shamata and Vipassana, we're abiding in the true nature of it all. But with Shamata, even though you're abiding in the true nature, you don't understand it—you see it but don't comprehend it. With Vipassana, you're both seeing it *and* comprehending what you're seeing.

Now perhaps you can understand why there are two parts to Vipassana:

1. Establishing by the supreme knowledge of analysis
2. Resting in the Way of Abiding* (or Nature of Mind)

FIRST THE FIRST ONE: ANALYSIS

Maybe I could explain this a wee bit more. When Rinpoche first began teaching me meditation, I asked him what to do when my mind followed after thoughts, making a whole movie. He said, "You can do either of two things: look directly at the thought, or look directly at the thinker." He took me on a whole adventure, looking at something on the outside. Then we went on another, looking at myself, the "thinker," as an inside phenomenon.

---

* Tib., *ne-luk*

Ever-changing Montana skies and landscapes

LOOKING AT THE THOUGHT-OTHER-OUTER

First, the outside. Rinpoche took the example of a mountain. We call it a mountain, but what is it, *exactly*, that we're calling a mountain? Is it the trees? The rocks? The vegetation? If we take away the vegetation, is it still a mountain? Let's focus on one part of the mountain: a tree. If we take some leaves off of it, or even a whole branch, is it still a tree? Is it the bark that contains the tree-ness? Let's analyze this some more. What we're calling "bark" is made up of lots of little cells. Have we gotten down to the real "mountain" yet? Or the "tree"?

We might say that the DNA of the cell is the tree part. We'll forget for a minute, the other parts without which the tree would die.

Let's break this down even further. Now we come to the level of molecules, then atoms. What's left of "tree-ness" when it's just a bunch of electrons, protons, and neutrons? Science tells us that there's proportionally as much space between the parts of the atoms as between the planets of our solar system. And scientists also tell us that when we get to the subatomic level, we can't even be sure they're *things*, *particles* anymore. As I mentioned in Book 1, there's been a debate among scientists as to whether these quantum building blocks are particles or waves. I personally wish they would've settled on calling them by one of the terms floating around as they discovered this minute level: "wavicles." They didn't consult me, and moved on to calling it "wave-particle." Boring.

If we were traveling with an infinitesimally small lens, we could pass through that "solid" tree, no problem. Continuing our journey using this tiny lens, we could pass from the inside of the tree to the outside of the tree, and not even notice the difference. We would mostly pass through space, waving at the occasional wave-particle outside our window. At this level, there's really no detectable difference between the thing we were calling a tree, and the rocks and air around it, never mind the mountain! David Bohm (remember him from Book 1?) might say that we've moved past the explicate and are staring at the implicate. The Buddha would say we have now used Sublime Insight—Vipassana—to look into the true nature of phenomena as they appear outside of us.

The ego can get a bit rattled at experiencing reality much closer to its true Way of Abiding. After all, the ego has a vested interest in being a separate, distinct thing. But at the same time, this is what we've been longing for, for untold ages: home.

Once we arrive HOME, why not rest there for a bit? Eventually a bit longer. Then longer. Gently, gradually extend that delicious moment of true rest, in true home. Rest in Shamata until you notice you've been following thoughts (again!). Do this analysis with whatever you've just thought about.

Are you ready to try this analysis for yourself? When you are, bring this section of the book into your Round Robin session—into the Shamata session in particular. We also have recordings of me leading this, on our website Namchak.org. See what you actually experience, as you fix your gaze of Sublime Insight on a thought or thing—your object of support, or a "distraction" such as that lady's pencil scratchings behind me. As you look into its true nature, what do you find? If you'd like me to talk you through it, go to our website. Better yet, go to a Vipassana retreat taught by Namchak Khen Rinpoche. He is Tulku Sangak Rinpoche's brother, and an accomplished scholar and meditator. He also happens to be a skilled and delightful teacher and inspiring human being. Again, there are also the other groups I mentioned earlier.

If all this seems a bit far-fetched, consider another example that Rinpoche gives us, from everyday life: a floater, those faint little things in your eye, that appear to be "out there." But in that case we know they're not. A classic Buddhist example is a person with jaundice thinking the world is yellow. We accept those differences between appearance and what's inherently *real*. Why not these

> The more our view aligns with true reality, the happier we'll be.

other examples? We're not in the habit of seeing a mountain or tree as non-solid. But as we consider and observe again and again, living with and getting used to that perspective, we might live increasingly

Namchak Khen Rinpoche in an action pose in Montana

Springtime in western Montana

from that perspective. And remember, the extent to which our view of reality differs from true reality is the extent to which we'll suffer. The reverse is also true: the more our view aligns with true reality, the happier we'll be.

ANOTHER OUTER ANALYSIS

We tend to assume that the things outside us are separate, and stably existing. We thought that mountain was. There's another, fascinating journey we can go on, to examine the "reality" of outer things. We can examine them from the point of Relative Truth.

Many years ago, I bought a beautiful wooden shrine cabinet for Rinpoche, for his room in Nepal. It was intricately carved, brightly painted in jewel tones, and trimmed in gold leaf. He was delighted with it, and put his most sacred scriptures, offering bowls, statues of enlightened beings, and other such things on and in it. He had representations of the Three Jewels contained in this lovely cabinet—the statues were bodies, the scriptures were speech, and the stupa was a sacred geometrical symbol of enlightened mind. He prostrated in the direction of this shrine every day.

Then he began to notice that someone else was enjoying his shrine, but in a very different way. It was quickly being perforated by termites! They found it delicious! They lived in, ate, and pooped in the shrine all day and all night.

From his point of view, the shrine's purpose was to hold the Three Jewels, and the termites were committing a sacrilege. From their point of view, it was a new home, with plenty to eat. But at the same time he thought, "Who's to say who's right? If this were a democratic process and we were to take a vote, I'd lose! The Buddha, who can see this from Absolute Truth, as well as from both of our points of view (Relative Truth), would agree with both of us." We humans could never eat the shrine if we tried. The termites eat nothing else. Is it food? A home to live in? Something to hold sacred objects and books? To some dogmatically zealous non-Buddhists, the shrine cabinet might be seen as an affront to their beliefs, a sacrilege to be destroyed. To a very poor, freezing non-Buddhist, it might be seen as firewood.

You get the idea. Even within this Samsaric dream, from different beings' perspectives, it's something very different. What is it, *really?* You can see why we call this *Relative* Truth. One or another appearance—shrine, lunch, home, Devil's work, or firewood—is true only relative to the observer.

Then there's the whole fascinating question of dreams. Rinpoche wrote a whimsical, yet profound allegory of a debate between waking and dreaming consciousness. Of course, Daytime (waking consciousness) asserted that it was more real. To give you a bit of a summation/paraphrase of the conversation: Night Time (dreaming consciousness) said, "When you go to sleep and experience a dream, isn't that just as real?"

"No, of course not. You have to wake up from a dream."

"Well, you have to go to sleep. Then you're in my realm. Besides, when you die, you'll have to wake up and leave that longer dream you call 'real life.'"

The debate went on like this, without either being able to show their view to be the right one. As I sat by my father's bed during the last month of his life, his senses

> "Peace, peace! He is not dead, he doth not sleep/ He hath awakn'd from the dream of life"
>
> *From "Adonais: An Elegy on the Death of John Keats" by Percy Bysshe Shelley*

withdrew. His vehicle for participating in this dream was falling apart, and he was going to have to go. Who knows where he went?

And when we experience one of those now-familiar movies while on the cushion, where do those thoughts go? Where exactly did they come from?

When you notice a thought on the internal screen of your mind, rather than getting engrossed in the internal video, what if you look *directly* at it? What happens? For me, when I catch it in the act like that, it goes "poof." It's like it was a balloon, popped by the sharp, direct observation of my mind. Or like a thief when the homeowner turns on the light. They slip away. Where do they go? Who knows? But now we're not caught in a movie. Now, once again, we're ready to rest in simple awareness. Whether a thought comes or not, no problem. We can *use* that thought as the object of our practice and simply look directly at it. Poof. Rest. Ahh.

> "Well, you have to go to sleep. Then you're in my realm. Besides, when you die, you'll have to wake up and leave that longer dream you call 'real life.'"

From all these various angles, we can see that the phenomena we perceive, whether "things" or dreams or thoughts, are woven together into a coherent story in our minds. They have no inherent existence without the mind. This is what's meant by the term "no-self" in Buddhism. Well then, shall we look right at that mind, the thinker?

LOOKING AT THE THINKER

As we're sitting there meditating, our brains are going to generate thoughts. No secret there! Rinpoche used a popular Tibetan Buddhist metaphor for how we can work with them. When you throw a stick, the dog will go after the stick. A lion will go after the thrower of the stick. We're now going to be lions. Going after the thinker is not for the fainthearted, as you will see. (It's more for the lionhearted, so to speak.) But inquiring minds want to know!

When a thought comes, we'll use it as a cue to look at the thinker by turning that same Vipassana lens directly on it—that is, on us. In addition to the great investigation-of-truth journey we're on, this process has a very practical application. When I'm lost in thought, on the cushion, I can take Rinpoche's second piece of advice and turn the analytical lens inward, onto the thinker. Who/what is this thinker anyway? As you've seen throughout these practices and contemplations, the Buddha has challenged our unconscious assumptions about what it's all about, and how it all works. One big assumption is about our very selves: how, and even whether, we exist. We could just go on assuming everything as before. But as you've seen by now, that could lead to a lot of suffering.

Near the beginning of this book, we talked about what this "I" might really be . . . and not be. Of the categories of "listen, contemplate, meditate," that was the "listen" one. I hope you've contemplated it a bit, and will continue to. Now you're going to actually gain direct experience with it, in meditation. Remember that the Tibetan word for "practice," *nyam-len,* means "to gain experience."

THE "WHAT'S LEFT" EXERCISE

Bringing this out of the intellectual and into your direct experience can be a bit hair-raising. Maybe you didn't realize you could have scary experiences while sitting on a cushion meditating. You can. The fundamental truth that we're terrified to admit is that our bodies don't exist as a substantial *thing.* Our minds aren't the stable things we think they are either. As you watch the flow of your thoughts and feelings, and turn the lens on the thinker, you begin to experience how insubstantial and ever-changing this tenuous "I" is. We do a lot of what we do, to distract ourselves from that fact; to bargain or negate that fact. Yet deep down we secretly know it to be true. Let me take you by the hand and step you to the edge and peer into that truth. Be gentle with yourself and take it in sips until you adjust to it a bit.

One small sip might be to think back on who you were ten years ago. You weren't quite the same person as you are today. How about five years ago? Do you think you'll be exactly the same next year? Might you not change just a little bit in even shorter periods of time? Might you be like a river, that's constantly changing as it flows along? In that case, who *are* you? You might try sitting with that for some of your Shamata/Vipassana sessions for a while.

Years ago, when Vipassana was my main practice, my favorite method of "looking at the thinker" was a particular exercise that took away all that wasn't "me," to see what was left. The time that this naturally happens for all of us is at death. So I rehearsed my own death. Of course this also serves well for the practice of Impermanence. Again, this is not for the fainthearted . . . but it's a really good glimpse into the truth. Again, the more we're living at odds with the truth the more we suffer. The more we live along with it, the happier we are. I find that any worry I have, that's secretly looming from behind, is actu-

> . . . the minute you conquer the fear of death, at that moment you are free.
>
> *Dr. Martin Luther King, Jr.*

ally more scary than when I bring it right out in front and take a good look. As Dr. Martin Luther King, Jr., noted, "I submit to you tonight no man is free if he fears death. But the minute you conquer the fear of death, at that moment you are free."

MY "LOOKING AT THE THINKER" PRACTICE

I begin by imagining I'm lying in a bed, no longer able to walk. I can't even go to the bathroom. So the "me" that is active, nimble, and rather athletic is gone.

Who/what am I? What's left?

Now I can't even lift my hands to grab the water glass or even gesture. What's left?

Now my senses of smell, taste, sight, and hearing become dim. What's left?

There go all those years of learning Tibetan. Who/what am I? What's left?

My skills as a psychotherapist, gone. What's left?

The piano lessons, singing. What's left?

My tendency to get lost even with the best of directions. What's left?

I see those and thousands of other "me" things all floating away. What's left?

The personality I identified as "I," is any of that left? It's my history and mental tendencies. Those leave too. What's left?

Even English.
Even being an American.
And even my name.
Gone.
What's left?

Perhaps it's my awareness. Just that—my awareness.

But what's this "my"? What container or boundary is there around this awareness?

I look, but I can't find one.

There's just awareness. Vast, universal awareness. It's not a vacuum, it's clear. It's pure potential for all and everything. It's unity. It's warm with pure, total connection—love. Joy.

This could be scary, but I find it beautiful. I'm actually reassured, that instead of death being a terrible/terrifying disappearing, it's just the imagined *boundaries* that disappear. It could be a joyful expanding beyond the tiny boundaries of who/what I thought I was . . . into the vast, ocean/heart. Here is an example that might give you a taste of that.

In the last act of the play *Our Town*, at the cemetery in Grover's Corners, the Stage Manager explains what happens to the dead after they are no longer among the living:

> *"Gradually, gradually, they lose hold of the earth . . . and the ambitions*
>   *they had . . . and the pleasures they had . . . and the things they*
>   *suffered . . . and the people they loved.*
> *They get weaned away from earth—that's the way I put it, weaned away.*
>   *And they stay here while the earth part of 'em burns away, burns*
>   *out; and all that time they slowly get indifferent to what's goin' on in*
>   *Grover's Corners.*
> *They're waitin'. They're waitin' for something that they feel is comin'.*
>   *Something important, and great. Aren't they waitin' for the eternal*
>   *part in them to come out clear?"*

THE SAME POINT

And so, whether we look at the thought or the thinker, we land on the same place. When we analyzed the tree, we couldn't find it. Likewise, when we dissected the "I," that slipped right through our fingers too. Normal appearances melted away, under the penetrating gaze of our Sublime Insight. From both directions we move past our habitual assumptions about "things out there" and/or "me in here," and land on a truer perception of reality. Free of old, habitual assumptions of how things are, we at least glimpse Absolute Truth: the underwater part of the iceberg, normally unseen, yet holding up the tip—Relative Truth. Harking back to our old favorite metaphor, we can now experience the deeper truth that the ocean and waves metaphor was pointing at. Only now it isn't just an intellectual exercise; through Vipassana, we've examined it, sat in it, and proven it for ourselves. Gradually that awareness can become our habitual way of seeing ourselves and the world.

ANOTHER WAY IN

We can also loosen our grip on this idea of a stable *ego* (which, you'll remember, is Latin for "I") from another direction. I'll talk more about this in the chapter in Book 4 on Impermanence, but for now you could just explore noticing how you think and feel different things every moment. As I touched on earlier, you can explore this conglomeration of thoughts, feelings, habits, personality traits/leanings, and how they shift and undulate. Give yourself the time to watch these shifting elements in action. I've sat by a river and watched it constantly changing, never the same from moment to moment. Then I let that be a model metaphor for my mind. What a wonderful exploration!

THE SHORT ANSWER TO THE OUTER

Rinpoche points out that, once we've proven to ourselves through close examination that the thinker isn't really, substantially, provably THERE, it logically follows that whatever the thinker was thinking (or perceiving) isn't really there either. Touché!

TWO POSSIBLE PITFALLS

First, some people have glimpsed the non-thingness of the thought and the thinker, and said in their minds, "This is emptiness." But that's still thing-izing emptiness. Ram Dass has talked about reaching such a moment in meditation, gleefully exclaiming, "Here I am! . . . wasn't I?" Oops.

Rather than saying, "This is it! I should stay here," let even that moment come and go. Let all the moments flow by, like a river. There's just awareness.

Second, it's okay to be aware of Relative Truth appearances—the surface appearance of things. In fact, to ignore Relative Truth is also seen as a mistake. The Buddha never said that appearances don't exist. It's the holding of the Two Truths together, without falling into allegiance to one versus another, that is the stance of the Middle Way. It's that seeming oxymoron of the ocean *and* the waves. Again, "not is, not isn't, not both, not neither." The Buddha expressed this in a famous essentialized rendering of the Heart Sutra:

Form is emptiness; emptiness is form. Form is not other than emptiness; emptiness is not other than form.

I like to say that slowly to myself, letting it peel away what I *think* form and emptiness are . . . leading me to something fresh and ineffable, that feels more like the truth. And again, Dharma means "truth."

There's a little book on the Heart Sutra, by Bokar Rinpoche and Khenpo Donyo*. In it they apply the Heart Sutra to each of the various sensory inputs. So it would be, "Sound is emptiness; emptiness is sound. Sound is not other than emptiness; emptiness is not other than sound." You can substitute "sights", "smells" (especially if your dog has indigestion), "sensations", and "taste." Especially bad taste. But no

---

* Bokar Rinpoche and Kenpo Donyo. *Profound Wisdom of the Heart Sutra and Other Teachings.* English Edition. California: ClearPoint Press, 1994.

SCIENCE TIDBIT

Meditation Cycle

By now you've no doubt gotten very familiar with the classic meditation progression: mind wandering, realizing your mind is wandering, bringing it back, maintaining focus. Around and around we go. One time I was in retreat, talking to a very advanced practitioner who had just finished her own retreat. I said, "No matter which practice I'm doing, it's all forgetting and remembering, forgetting and remembering." She laughed, "Yes, when we pass by each other in the *Bardo*, we'll say, 'You still forgetting and remembering?' 'Yep!'"

We aren't just wasting our time, going in circles. Dan Harris, news anchor and author of *10% Happier*, says that this cycle is like a bicep curl for your brain. In the laboratory at the University of Wisconsin, Dr. Richard Davidson and his colleagues have shown more precisely what that bicep curl looks like, in the brain.

Similar work is going on at Emory University, among other sites: in an article in the November 2014 issue of *Scientific American*, Dr. Davidson and his colleagues, Antoine Lutz, and Matthieu Ricard recount the findings of Dr. Wendy Hasenkamp from her work at Emory University.

Dr. Hasenkamp and her colleagues studied the four stages of the cycle I described above, capturing images of which areas of the brain become active at each stage. They were able to map out a consistent pattern. They were specifically studying "focused attention," which is a non-Buddhist term for the combination of Shamata and Vipassana that I've described above.

Posterior inferior parietal region

Posterior cingulate cortex

Precuneus

Medial prefrontal cortex

Lateral temporal cortex

1 **Mind Wandering**
Imaging of a meditator in the scanner illuminates the posterior cingulate cortex, the precuneus and other areas that are part of the default-mode network, which stays active when thoughts begin to stray.

When they were in the first phase—distracted wandering—the part of the brain that lit up was the "wide-ranging default-mode network (DMN)." Put an "A" in that and you get the word you might feel like saying when you realize you've been wandering. Again.

But wait! That's the second phase—*realizing* you were wandering. Now other areas light up, as you can see in the illustration. You just shifted to those desirable areas. No need to curse!

The third phase—bringing your mind back to the object of focus—activates the dorsolateral prefrontal cortex and the lateral inferior parietal lobe. Trust me, that's a good thing. We want to strengthen those areas and the pathways to them. Then we can get increasingly better at bringing our attention back once it's been distracted.

Wouldn't it be nice to hold it there, on whatever we want it to stay focused on? That's the last phase they studied. Indeed, the dorsolateral prefrontal cortex stays active as we keep our focus on the breath, image, or wherever we want our attention to be. Of course we do get distracted—i.e. going back to stage one of this four-stage cycle. But instead of permanently staying in stage one (which is what we did pretty much 24/7 before meditation), we move through the other stages. Much better to add the other three, wouldn't you say?

Anterior insula

Anterior cingulate cortex

3 Reorientation of Awareness
Two brain areas—the dorsolateral prefrontal cortex and the inferior parietal lobe—are among those that help to disengage attention from a distraction to refocus on the rhythm of the inhalations and exhalations.

2 Distraction Awareness
The salience network, which includes the anterior insula and the anterior cingulate cortex, underlies the meditator's awareness of the distraction.

Inferior parietal lobe

Dorsolateral prefrontal cortex

4 Sustaining Focus
The dorsolateral prefrontal cortex stays active when the meditator directs attention on the breath for long periods.

Dorsolateral prefrontal cortex

need to stop there. You can also do it with "feelings" (the emotional kind) and "thoughts." The Tibetans see us as having six avenues of perception, with thinking being one of them. I see their point. What a great tool, for dealing with thoughts on the cushion! . . . not that we have any of those . . .

Instead of seeing these as mere distractions to drop, you can see any of them as a means to bring yourself back to the Way of Abiding.

RESTING

Through analyzing either the thought or the thinker, we fall into the most pure and accurate, direct perception of the truth that we can. With Vipassana, now we not only *see* it clearly, as we do in Shamata; we comprehend it. Now the only thing left to do, as I've said before, is to . . .

Rest in that state. Shamata.

And just in case we can't rest for very long, once we notice we're in a mind-movie again, we can use Vipassana to find our way back out of the movie. Then we land in a *fresh* state of cognizant abiding. Now that you've analyzed using Vipassana, you have a better understanding of that resting/abiding state. Each time we realize we're distracted, we *use* that distraction by applying Vipassana to it. We find our way home and settle back into that state, resting in it. Again we get distracted. Around and around we go. Slowly, after resting in this Shamata/Vipassana more and more, we'll come to trust that experience, and live from it more and more. We gradually come to more and more profound realization of that "home base."

> Once we notice we're in a mind-movie again, we can use Vipassana to find our way back out of the movie.

Other studies have found that the parts of the brain involved in the realizing, remembering, and re-settling phases seemed to benefit, in two ways. First, some of the critical parts of the brain that become active in these phases grew measurably bigger and/or denser. Some of those parts that enlarged usually shrink with age, but in older meditators they held their size (though

> The wider the gap,
> the more misery;
> the smaller the gap,
> the less misery.

they didn't get bigger). Second, the connections between desirable parts and other parts of the brain increased. The following Science Tidbit gives a bit of an overview of this.

Now that I've gone into some of the benefits to your brain, I want to circle back to the benefit for your life experience. After all, the end goal isn't just to light up different parts of your brain; it's to be a better, happier person. Or for some of us overachievers, totally waking up like the Buddha! We could boil it down to this: if true reality is one thing, and our understanding of it is another, that gap will be a source of misery, for us and those around us.

The wider the gap, the more misery; the smaller the gap, the less misery.

The closing of the gap was the Buddha's intent. His methods help us to do just that. I hope this practice lessens the gap, lessens the misery, clearing the way for much more happiness. I believe that's our

YET ANOTHER SCIENCE TIDBIT
Mindfulness and Brain Change

The *Harvard Business Review* article "Mindfulness Can Literally Change Your Brain,"* by Christina Congleton, Britta K. Hölzel, and Sara W. Lazar, talks of the changes in brain functions that act as the "proof in the pudding" of meditation. Well, from one angle. The two neuroscientists and one psychologist give a bit of an overview of the research on this subject. They go into some detail about three beneficial well-documented brain changes, and generally point to others. The first is in the anterior cingulate cortex (ACC), just behind the brain's frontal lobe. Self-regulation (consciously directing your attention) and holding off on knee-jerk reactions are associated with this area. A second benefit is mental flexibility. This latter function has to do not just with this area of the ACC itself, but also with the strength of the pathways between it and other parts of the brain. Meditators showed better performance in all of the above capacities, and their ACC showed more activity than non-meditators.

As if that weren't enough to make us love the ACC, it's associated with a third benefit of learning from experience to make good decisions. I'll take two! Oh wait, I already *have* two—one on each side. So do you. Now to meditate and make them stronger . . .

The other brain region poster child in this article was the hippocampus. Despite its name it's actually quite small. If you were to travel two-thirds of the way between your temple and the very middle of your brain, you'd encounter this seahorse-shaped part. It's associated with emotion and memory. In people suffering from post-traumatic stress disorder (PTSD) and other stress-related problems like depression, it becomes smaller. But in meditators the gray matter in that area increased! This points to resilience, which is a trump card in life, if you ask me.

true, natural state. I believe that the natural state of true reality is extremely joyful.

So . . . to come at it from another way . . .

The more our vision of reality matches true reality, the happier we are.

The more our vision of reality matches true reality, the happier we are.

They sum up the research in this field further by saying, "These findings are just the beginning of the story. Neuroscientists have also shown that practicing mindfulness affects brain areas related to perception, body awareness, pain tolerance, emotion regulation, introspection complex thinking, and sense of self. While more research is needed to document these changes over time and to understand underlying mechanisms, the converging evidence is compelling."*

So that's a very fancy way of validating Dan Harris' claim about bicep curls for the brain.

Furthermore, as has been proven in various studies including the Shamatha (different spelling of "Shamata') Project (Clifford Saron, et al), as we practice, we get better at the "remembering" (i.e. "Oh yeah, I was practicing") part. So if you're doing a lot of forgetting and remembering as you practice, well done! Really, this all makes sense. The more you do something, the better you get at it. The more bicep curls, the stronger the bicep. I should hasten to add that you can't make your ACC grow infinitely bigger—to Arnold Schwarzenegger bicep size, for example. Brain parts just don't grow that big. But findings have consistently shown the ACC and other parts to grow measurably, even within weeks of beginning meditation.

Interestingly, scientists such as Davidson and some of his colleagues, who have studied meditation masters for decades, suspect that after such processes become deep, default habits (think "unconscious competence," like riding a bicycle or reading these words), those brain parts become normal size again. This idea hasn't been thoroughly studied yet, in the new field of contemplative science.

---

* Sara W. Lazar, Britta K. Holzel, and Christina Congleton. "Mindfulness Can Literally Change Your Brain," Harvard Business Review (digital), January 8, 2015, https://hbr.org/2015/01/mindfulness-can-literally-change-your-brain

PRACTICING THIS PRACTICE

As you'd probably guessed, you'll incorporate this approach into your daily Round Robin sessions. If you've already spent months doing Shamata daily, then hopefully you've stabilized your mind enough that you're ready to begin to fold Vipassana in with the Shamata sections of your Round Robin. If not, then do yourself a BIG favor and wait until you've got a more stable foundation in Shamata. I really encourage you to have a strong, stable foundation before building on it; otherwise you'll end up with something like the Leaning Tower of Pisa. I don't think you want to do that with your mind.

Once you've determined you're ready, I suggest you re-read the whole Vipassana section. Then you can fold it into your practice. And

I can't recommend highly enough that you go to at least a weekend Vipassana retreat. In his book, *10% Happier,* Dan Harris talks of reading and reading about Buddhism. But it isn't until he road-tests meditation that he begins to experience real personal benefits. Then he signs up for a Vipassana retreat. At first, he goes rather stir-crazy (like, as I mentioned earlier, Daniel Siegel at his first retreat). Harris regales us with a blow-by-blow account of his mind on the cushion. Hysterical! Then his mind settled down.

That retreat changed his life.

SUMMARY

- When you come to the Shamata part of the Round Robin, rest in Shamata.

- When you notice you've been lost in thoughts, look *directly at* the thought and analyze it to see its lack of intrinsic existence (Vipassana). Or just look directly at it and watch it go poof. Or look at the *essence* of the thinker. You might do the dying rehearsal sometimes.

- Recognize that truth that you land on, with certainty.

- Immediately rest in Shamata. Remember, you're not stopping thoughts, simply registering them as they flow by.

- If you do this many times per session, *good!* Many reps for your brain and mind! Lots of glimpsing the true nature of thoughts and thinker, and lots of fresh resting back in Shamata.

When you're bored with resting, or drowsy, or realize you've been sunk in a mind movie, bring analytical meditation (Vipassana) again (following the above steps), until you realize the true nature of whatever you're analyzing, with confidence. This is a way to alternate Shamata with Vipassana.

During these next few months (or longer), I suggest you use the following Round Robin guideline, emphasizing the analytical Vipassana or catching the thought in the act (and resting once you've arrived at the ultimate point of the analysis or it's gone poof) until you've thoroughly developed certainty. If you can attend at least one Vipassana or Shamata retreat during this time, it would hugely help your practice. Better yet, both!

FOLLOW-THROUGH

You might think that now you know how to do Vipassana. It's tempting to think that. After all, how can you know what you still don't know? That's why I want to be sure to remind you: as with everything in this whole *Smiling* series, I'm just giving you an introduction to the different concepts and practices, to give you a way to get started. With Vipassana too, there's a *ton* more to know, and you can follow a progression to further train your mind. What might be the next stages? Well, of course, how can you know about the rest of it until you, well, know the rest of it? And that gets to be a long story best heard in person. Every year, we offer a four-part series of weekend retreats, starting with Shamata and progressing through three levels of Vipassana, taught by Namchak Khen Rinpoche. He's a scholar of the highest level, in the Nyingma tradition, as well as a consummate practitioner. He's also a powerful lama. Surprisingly, even though he needs a translator for the teachings, he's an accessible teddy bear, bringing lots of jokes and stories to illustrate the teachings. We tend to find the retreats by turns funny, fascinating, peaceful, and mind-blowing.

Namchak Khen Rinpoche at site for Three-Year Retreat with the Mission Mountain Range behind him

Sample Daily Practice Session #2
ROUND ROBIN MEDITATION WITH VIPASSANA AND THE FOUR
BOUNDLESS QUALITIES

- **1 MINUTE OR LESS:** Check motivation for doing this practice, in this session. Bring forward Bodhisattva motivation (the Two Purposes) if necessary. (Remember: it almost always needs a little bringing forward, but don't expect it to be one hundred percent before moving on—that's what the practice is *for*, after all.) Remember, because of the holographic nature of reality, your efforts to wake up really do help us all, to do that. And you probably have important, more local reasons too. What are they in *this* session?

- **1 MINUTE:** Clearing the Stale Energies Rest

- **10 TO 15 MINUTES:** Shamata/Vipassana

- **5 TO 10 MINUTES:** Equanimity, Loving Kindness, Compassion (Tonglen), or Sympathetic Joy (pick one)

- **5 MINUTES:** Shamata/Vipassana

  At this point, you might want to gradually push the envelope on the time you spend on each step in the Round Robin. Bulk up those brain biceps! It doesn't matter which of the two Shamata/Vipassana parts is the long one. You decide.

- **30 SECONDS:** Dedication of merit and aspirational prayers.

DEDICATION AND ASPIRATION

By the power of this compassionate practice
May suffering be transformed into peace.
May the hearts of all beings be open,
And their wisdom radiate from within.

(Courtesy of the *Tergar Sangha*)

Post Meditation

Here's a way to increase the benefits of your meditation time exponentially: apply them to life. We talked about that in relation to the Four Boundless Qualities, and it's also true with Vipassana. In fact, the two dovetail nicely, in supporting your efforts to wake up to reality as it actually is. After your session, as you look at the world of various appearances around you, apply your newfound, deeper understanding of their nature—in other words, see them as dreamlike—not so separate and solid as they once seemed. Apply this view to that famous nursery rhyme and really notice the words, "Row, row, row your boat gently down the stream. Merrily, merrily, merrily, merrily, life is but a dream." It's an anthem for Vipassana practitioners—who knew? One natural response to this is compassion for all the beings who don't have this understanding. As you rest in the essential nature of you, of it all, notice that a quality of that nature is love, compassion. So Shamata/Vipassana leads us to the same destination that the Four Boundless Qualities lead us to . . . just from a different angle.

> *One who enters an emptiness devoid of compassion*
> *Has not found the supreme of paths.*
> *When compassion alone is cultivated,*
> *One remains here in Samsara, so liberation is not attained.*
> *For those who are able to unite the two,*
> *They will not remain in Samsara, nor dwell in Nirvana.*

Rather, they can eventually reach full enlightenment—awakening. Once again, wisdom and compassion together.

Lojong—SEVEN POINT MIND TRAINING

I mentioned this very briefly in Book 2, then talked it up in the Recommended Reading list in the back. In the Post-Meditation (the other 23½ hours of the day) department, I've found it to be one of my best supports in this business of waking up. Doing a few minutes of meditation in the morning, then jumping up and doing your life in "business as usual" mode won't be the most efficient way to make

---

* Saraha

progress. Of course we all want to manifest these changes in our lives, then return to the cushion tomorrow having actually made progress having used the experiences of our everyday lives. But how?

Lojong! In Tibetan that means "Mind Training." Perhaps the most well-known and popular in Tibet (with good reason) is the one compiled by Geshe Chekawa Yeshe Dorje. No one really knows who wrote the first version or when, but over the centuries, many masters have written various versions and commentaries. The one I've fallen in love with and know best is the Chekawa Yeshe Dorje version. He first stumbled upon a version of it written by Atisha, a great Bengali master who had spent years studying under Serlingpa in Indonesia. Serlingpa wrote an earlier version. Chekawa happened to see Atisha's version sitting on a friend's daybed. He glimpsed one of its maxims about: "Give all victory to others; take all defeat for yourself."

Chekawa was intrigued. To be honest, when I first came to that maxim and was to go through the day with that as my theme, I was annoyed. "*Why* do I have to do that?" I whined inwardly. It's the opposite of what we try to do. So are many of the maxims. I decided to try it anyway, thinking, "I've tried it my way for countless eons, and where has it gotten me? Might as well try something else." In a discussion/debate I was having with a co-worker, I decided to see if I could find some point she was making, drop my opposing point, and acknowledge she was right. Amazingly enough, I found it. Turns out, when I drop the need to see it only my way, my ferocious grip on I/me/mine loosens just a bit. And I actually *learn* something too. Who knew?! As time went on, I found other victories I could give to others. To my surprise I felt good about it, and naturally the other person felt happy too. By the end of that day, I didn't want to move on to the next maxim. I generally find myself wanting to work with a maxim for three days to a week. And I've gone through the whole list of them (more than fifty!) several times.

Back to Chekawa. Seeing the value of applying these very practical little maxims to life, he devoted himself to studying it deeply. For twelve years. Then he compiled the Seven Point Mind Training, which became widely practiced and loved, throughout all lineages of Tibet. This was something not just for lamas, but for anyone who had challenges in life and might want to turn them into opportunities for happiness, mastering life despite challenges, and even using the challenges to wake up.

Later, a leader in the *Rimey* (ecumenical) movement of the nineteenth century, Jamgön Kongtrül the Great, wrote the commentary that I found my way to. It was translated by Ken McLeod. Pema
Chödrön does a wonderful, modern Western-style commentary in her
book, *Start Where You Are*. It's very real and accessible.

There are many commentaries on this version of the Seven Point
Mind Training. I'll re-list them for you in the Recommended Reading
section in the back of this book. Since making that list, I've created a
little audio commentary for the app called Happify. It's in the form of
a "track," which is made up of four weeks' worth of daily installments,
usually ten to fifteen minutes long. In mine I introduce a maxim, talk
about it for a few minutes, then lead a few minutes of meditation. I was
hoping to help people start their day with it, and carry the maxim with
them as their theme for the day. That's just what I did myself, with the
Seven Point Mind Training, and I loved it. I wanted to share it with you
so you could bring the benefits of meditation into your day. In turn,
the benefits of applying the maxims to challenges in your life will help
you on the cushion.

Jamgön Kongtrül the Great

Students in pairs digesting the teachings together

CONCLUSION

Sangha—Meditating and Ruminating with Friends

Of course there are lots of ways to bring the realizations and experiences on the cushion into daily life. Explore! Explore it with a friend and co-conspirator! I call it a Meditation Buddy. We offer Toolkits you and your Buddy can use together, for more ideas. Many people have started small (living-room size) meditation/study groups we call Learning Circles. The Toolkit works for those too.

Learning Circles and Meditation Buddies can be a perfect balance to solo meditating. It reminds me of the little school orchestra I was in, as a kid. If I didn't practice the violin at home, it was going to sound like a screeching cat in rehearsals and performances. So I did practice a bit at home. Equally important was practicing all together. Otherwise the whole effect was still going to be painful. Okay, it was a little painful anyway, but trust me, before rehearsals it was a lot worse! Rehearsal time was also a chance to see if anyone was practicing their part wrong, setting in the wrong patterns. That, and playing too loud or soft, all comes out in rehearsing together.

Likewise, in the presence of others who are maybe also practicing Lojong, you can create a learning laboratory together. If someone feels pain from something another said or did, it can be a safe place to practice NVC, Lojong, or just saying "Ouch!" The other person, and the group, can work it through with you—such a rare and precious option these days. You also have the opportunity to explore your own sore spots and "emotional allergies," to see if it was more from your side than theirs. In the context of Sangha, you can say "ouch" and explain about your sore spots. In that context you can get some real support. We developed those sore spots in relationship, and healing can also happen in relationship—maybe most effectively.

After working together on such things, as well as your inner and outer adventures with these methods in the face of your lives, real warmth of deep friendship develops. I've heard so many people say, "I don't have another place, even with my family, where I can connect so deeply and satisfyingly with people." To tell you the truth, I'm not much of a joiner, myself. But even I have found such connection deeply satisfying. I can see why the Buddha made Sangha one of the Three Jewels needed for totally waking up.

I believe that we human beings want to be active in three areas in our lives: personal, community, and the world. If you've read this far, I'm sure you already feel the need to pursue a rich inner personal life. Yet how much time can we devote to developing our inner life, given how much modern life demands we spend time in outer pursuits?

Most of us do want to be a part of a "beloved community," as Dr. King called it. Yet we don't spend much time at that either. Again, when we get through doing what we have to do for work and family, how much time do we have for community? But if we don't spend time

> People will send flowers to your funeral, but won't bring you soup when you're sick.

with our friends, nurture those friendships, how can those bonds strengthen and deepen? As the wry saying goes, "People will send flowers to your funeral, but won't bring you soup when you're sick."

Most of us feel we'd love to help our wider community, our country, or our world, but feel daunted by knowing where to begin, or what will really help. That's something that you and your Meditation Buddy, or your Learning Circle, could discuss together. I bet others also want to do something but might not know where to start either. You can all trade off being the speaker who ruminates aloud on what they feel called to do, and the listener who supports the speaker in the inquiry. Better yet if there's a third person to act as a witness, to write notes, notice some overarching theme, or add a reflection at the end.

I just outlined three roles in something called the Partnering Exercise, developed by Aaron Stern at the Academy for the Love of Learning®, which he founded. We like to use that exercise for this and a general way of deepening connection in Learning Circles, as well as bringing real benefit to all three people. For more information and a little booklet to guide you through the process, you can go to the Academy website: aloveoflearning.org. Much better would be to attend one of our weekend seminars where Aaron teaches it. In just that short time, people bond deeply because he's essentialized and highlighted how we humans do supportive conversation, in our better moments.

I feel I also have to give a word to the wise here: I've never seen someone meditate only on their own for very long. If they aren't connecting with others, comparing notes about their on-and-off-the-cushion experiences, studying together, and meditating together regularly, people just trail off. I found out more recently that there's a lot of science to back that up. Charles Duhigg provides us with plenty in his book, *The Power of Habit*.* Perhaps even more compelling is all the science in the book, *Connected: The Surprising Power of Our Social Networks and How They Shape Our Lives—How Your Friends' Friends' Friends Affect Everything*

---

*   Duhigg, Charles. *The Power of Habit: Why We Do What We Do in Life and Business.* New York: Random House Trade Paperbacks, an imprint of Random House, a division of Random House LLC, a Penguin Random House Company, 2012, 2014.

You Feel, Think, and Do, by Nicholas Christakis and James Fowler.* That long subtitle tells you a bit about some surprising statistics around just how much we're affected by people—sometimes people we don't even know because they're affecting us through our friends.

GROUP MEDITATION—WHY BOTHER?

I've mentioned this metaphor above, but now I'm asking you to recall: have you ever practiced music or sung alone, then played (or sung) with others? Quite different experiences, playing alone versus playing or singing with others. I love both! It's similar with meditation. In solo music and meditation, you can do it just the way you like, doing each part as long or as short as you like, and there's such a peaceful quality (when it's going well!). But something else gets to happen in a group. When I've meditated with others, the power of all of us doing the same thing at the same time boosts us all to another level. I think of it as our "infecting" each other with the feeling/experience. In fact, in Vajrayana they say that it's difficult to reach full enlightenment without practicing with others. And I thought it was already difficult!

Why would they say that? Think of the power of group thinking and views. Have you ever been to an inspiring political rally or demonstration? A rock concert? A rousing football game? Or on the negative side, think of a Ku Klux Klan rally or even a lynching. Probably no one in any of those examples would feel so strongly if it weren't for the tide of group feeling/thinking/views that carry us along. Every year at the Buddha Garden, we do something very popular in Tibet called a *drupchöd,* or Group Accomplishment. It's a weeklong group meditation. We're chanting the same thing together at the same time for several sessions a day, visualizing what the liturgy is talking about, and progressing through a kind of story, all together. It's like the difference between ambient light and laser light. The waves in ambient light go up and down randomly, while the waves in laser light go up and down together—hence the term "coherent light." We all know how powerful coherent light—laser light—is. In drupchöds, we fall into coherent

---

*   Christakis, Nicholas A. and Fowler, James H. *Connected: The Surprising Power of Our Social Networks and How They Shape Our Lives.* New York: Little, Brown and Co., Hachette Book Group, 2011.

Lama Tsomo demonstrating a practice with one student

thought/feeling/view/experience. It's quite powerful in helping us to quickly loosen our usual grip/fixation on this "channel" of reality and open up to a more pure level.

The very purpose of Vajrayana is to purify our vision—clear and straighten our warped, splattered windshield. Or to go with another analogy I like, we help each other to "change channels" of reality.

And remember David Bohm, in his conversation with Renée Weber? In his own way, he was talking about how, as we purify our vision, then band together with others who are doing the same, the power of our vision increases exponentially. Then we really have hope of inoculating the group consciousness of humanity to move the needle toward waking up. That's so sorely needed these days. If we all woke up, we wouldn't harm each other or the environment because we would know in our bones that we're all in this soup together.

I'm obviously not a conservative Christian, but I applaud Rick Warren and the Saddleback Church because in their small groups, they all encourage each other not just to inner work, but to go out and manifest whatever good that each person feels called to do in the world. Then in their little Sunday groups, they all tell their stories and support each other in that work.

All of which is to say that, despite my not being a joiner, I'm recommending you consider treading this path with at least one other fellow journeyer, and going to in-person retreats whenever you can. All of that will give you a huge boost, and continually refresh your practice. It's easy to look online for retreats. But how might you find someone to practice with regularly, to keep your practice alive and progressing? You could look at our Toolkit for ideas, and contact us in case there's someone in your area, or at least online, who's looking for someone too. Or talk a friend into it! Here's hoping you find support for your practice in Sangha!

What's Next?

A whole lot, as it happens. Once you've spent about a year doing Shamata, Vipassana, and the Four Boundless Qualities, you're ready for a group of practices called Ngöndro, meaning "Go-Before" or "Preliminary." You're probably thinking, "It seems like it's going *after.*" There are a couple of reasons for thinking of them as preliminary. First, once you incorporate a bit at a time into your daily practice, you'll still finish your session with Shamata/Vipassana, so these "Preliminary Practices" will indeed "go before." Second, the five Preliminary Practices, altogether, take you through a microcosm of the whole Vajrayana path to enlightenment—each of the major stages in essentialized form.

For the rest of this *Ancient Wisdom for Our Times* series we'll focus on the Ngöndro. By the end, you'll have an introduction and beginning practice guidelines for all of its stages. Though it will be helpful to have them in hand, you'll absolutely need to go to in-person retreats, at that level. The Ngöndro is the stage at which Vajrayana moves beyond the practices that all branches of Buddhism share. The medicine gets increasingly strong—kind of like moving to prescription medicine or very strong herbs—and you need an experienced doctor/herbalist to benefit from them and avoid bad side effects. My purpose in writing this series is to give you a guidebook or beginning textbook for the Ngöndro, to refer to as you progress through it under the guidance of a qualified lama.

At the end of Book 2, I talked about the process of finding a qualified lama. The Buddha created the three Yanas, or branches of Buddhism, because he was aware that we're all different and need different approaches. This is really true within Vajrayana. One lineage

Lama Tsomo about to lead students in a practice at Grace Cathedral in San Francisco

or another might appeal more to you; one lama or another might feel more like home to you; one sangha or another as well. The good news about America in particular and modern life in general is that we have a whole smorgasbord to choose from.

A FEW CAUTIONARY WORDS
The bad news is that we have that whole smorgasbord so we can get confused, waste time hopping from one "dish"—one path of awakening to the next—without making forward progress in any of them; or worst of all, mixing them together to create mush. Each of them has their own particular liturgies and subtle differences that work within their own systems. The benefit will be lost if you try to mix and match. That works fine with couches and pillows (though not always) but really doesn't work at this level of practice.

ROOT LAMA

One difference between Vajrayana and the other branches of Buddhism is that we use the Lama, the Guru, in a particular way. At the risk of stating the obvious, we have trouble seeing our own Buddha Nature, or we wouldn't be going through all this! Fortunately, we humans have this tendency to project unseen/unconscious parts of ourselves onto others. This can be terrible when it takes the form of scapegoating, as we all know. It can be wonderful if we use it to bring our Buddha Nature

> At the risk of stating the obvious, we have trouble seeing our own Buddha Nature, or we wouldn't be going through all this!

into view. When we enter into a Root Lama/student relationship, we and the lama agree that we're going to project our own Buddha Nature onto them until we can fully know and own it ourselves. I *hasten* to add that in every single session, we go through the process of projecting our buddha nature onto our Root Lama and taking it back into ourselves, sitting awhile in the unity of what we projected and our own true essence. Eventually we know our own Buddha Nature well, and can live from that.

The other reason why the lama is essential for us in Vajrayana is that the methods become like increasingly stronger medicines. Once you get into prescription medicine, you need a qualified doctor. For really strong medicine, you need to keep going to the doctor for testing and tweaking. The other thing is that, since it's our flawed ego that's working on our flawed ego, and our flawed mind working on our

> In every single session, we go through the process of projecting our buddha nature onto our Root Lama and taking it back into ourselves, sitting awhile in the unity of what we projected and our own true essence.

flawed mind, we need an experienced lama to see us from outside ourselves, and give us advice or a nudge in a needed direction.

As you might be guessing, this spiritual mentorship is a profound relationship. In future books we'll explore in much more depth how to do that relationship from our side, in practice as well as between sessions. If we do it correctly, we can use it to grow by leaps and bounds, reaching the point of living from our own true nature much more quickly. If we do it wrong, we can end up confused, miserable, and off track. While Vajrayana is a very efficient and direct path, as with any strong medicine, you have to approach with respect and skill. If you see the Root Lama/student relationship in much the way I've described above, you'll be on the right track to getting the benefits without stepping into the pitfalls. And, as with anything in life, it's always essential to use your good sense and trust your gut. Remember, blind faith is not a virtue in this path!

Just to be clear, although I'm an ordained lama, I'm not a candidate to be your Root Lama. Fortunately you have better options. In Namchak we have Tulku Sangak Rinpoche and his brother, Namchak Khen Rinpoche. They are far and away more qualified for you to project your Buddha Nature onto, and they're more experienced with guiding students than I am. As with any projection, you're looking for the most likely projection screen. That would be someone who has used these methods enough that they've purified their own vision and minds to be worthy projection screens.

I speak English and can introduce these stages of practice in terms that make sense to modern Westerners. Having been at this awhile, perhaps longer than you, I can act as a big sister. I've been offering that in these books, and in live, online meditation coaching calls. But with such great projection screens as those two lamas, why not go with the best? In your daily sessions, it doesn't matter if they don't speak English! You also don't have to hang out with them a lot. Just as people project onto musicians and actors, we don't even have to meet someone to have a strong projection on them. But with these lamas you can actually meet and get teachings from them. I highly recommend experiencing their teachings. Though they each have their own style, both are accessible, clear, and knowledgeable, not to mention entertaining!

Maybe you feel you need to go through the Vajrayana section of the smorgasbord, to see which lineage and lama best suits you. By all means! Once you've decided, and it turns out to be someone else, you'll need to go with their liturgy and instructions for their system of practices.

Preview of Book Four

If you decide to explore the next stage of this path, as I said, I'll begin teaching you the Ngöndro. Book Four will cover a preliminary stage (so a Preliminary to the Preliminaries!) and the first two practices. That's because they take you through a journey, sometimes in just a few minutes, that is a microcosm—a hologram?—of the whole Vajrayana path. Each section is a whole journey in itself, and people go for months, sometimes years doing each section in great depth. I spent a few months to a year on each one. At first I thought, "Will I *live* long enough to finish this whole thing? What more could I get out of this?" After I'd spent a bit more time with whatever section it was, it really opened up for me and I thought, "If I spent the rest of my life just doing this profound practice, it would be time well spent!" By the end I'd think, "But I haven't totally mastered this part. I'm not ready to move to the next one!" Desire/clinging—my favorite poison!

Luckily, you don't have to drop the practices you've already been doing. In fact, the Four Boundless Qualities are what you'll be practicing in the second section of the Ngöndro, and you'll practice Shamata/Vipassana at the end, so you've already got a head start! Also luckily, it didn't take me the rest of my life—it only took me about four years, while I finished raising my kids, did outer work, and even moved.

In any case, I wish you all the best in your practicing what we've covered in this volume. May your use of them bring you happiness, ease your suffering, and bring you the deep satisfaction of a meaningful life. As you, and perhaps you with a group of friends, wake up more and more, may you infect all the rest of us who are in this big soup together. If you find that you want to come to any of our programs, I hope to see you there!

Lama Tsomo

Appendix A: Glossary

Absolute Truth (Tibetan: *dön-dam-denba*): The abiding truth, not subject to a particular deluded being's point of view. The reality perceived by enlightened beings. *See also* Two Truths.

Archetype: Jungian term describing a sort of lens that acts as a template, shaping generalized consciousness into a more particular principle of reality with particular characteristics—for example, the Great Mother archetype or the Wise Man archetype—which one can find in images and stories throughout human societies.

Bardo (Tibetan; literally "between two"): Generally used to refer to the dreamlike state between lifetimes. Technically we experience other bardos, such as the time in between birth and death.

Bodhicitta [bo-di-CHIT-ta] (Sanskrit; "Mind of Enlightenment/Awakening"): "On the relative level, it is the wish to attain Buddhahood for the sake of all beings, as well as the practice of the path of love, compassion, the six transcendent perfections, etc., necessary for achieving that goal. On the absolute level, it is the direct insight into the ultimate nature." (From *The Words of My Perfect Teacher* by Patrul Rinpoche, trans., Padmakhara Translation Group.) It is the motivation to help others. It naturally flows from our own Buddha Nature, which *feels* how we're not separate from others.

Bodhisattva [bo-di-SAT-va] (Sanskrit): One who is primarily motivated by bodhicitta. There are many levels of bodhisattva, depending on the spiritual achievement of such a being.

Buddha (Sanskrit; "Awakened One"): A being who has reached full enlightenment by cleansing all adventitious *lo-bur* ("baggage"), such as karma and bad habits of the mind, and has fully brought forth—matured—their Buddha Nature. It is predicted that there will be over a thousand who will reach this state in this *kalpa*, or aeon. Note: The buddha who created the religion and methods of Buddhism and taught the sutras and tantras was the Buddha Shakyamuni.

Buddha Nature (Tibetan: *deshek nyingpo*): Our essential nature, which is not separate from the Dharmakaya and is the seed of our own complete enlightenment.

Dharma (Sanskrit): A general term for the teachings and path of the Buddha Shakyamuni.

Dharmakaya (Sanskrit; literally "Truth Body"): The vast, pregnant emptiness out of which everything arises. It is not a dead vacuum, but pure, essential awareness. It is beyond defining but has many qualities. It is vast without limit; ultimate compassion, ultimate unity, pure potential, all-knowing, the ultimate root of all. At this level there is no form; there is unity. It is no different from complete Buddhahood.

Dukka: A Sanskrit term that's usually translated as "suffering." But it's more like basic, baked-in unsatisfactoriness. People are increasingly referring to it in that latter way, which I believe is more accurate.

Five Dhyani Buddha Families: For each of these five categories, or families, there is a particular buddha, color, direction, and many other characteristics. These are the Sanskrit Buddha Family names (male, female).

1. Buddha: Vairochana, Dhatishvari
2. Lotus: Amitabha, Pandaravasini
3. Vajra: Akshobhya, Buddhalochana
4. Jewel: Ratnasambhava, Mamaki
5. Karma: Amogasiddhi, Samayatara

These are also listed in the same order as the Five Poisons (see below). The Five Buddha Families weave together, along with all their qualities and characteristics, to create the complex appearances of manifested reality.

Five Poisons: The five neurotic emotions that usually motivate the thoughts, speech, and actions of sentient beings. The Buddha spoke of 84,000 of them, but they are generally grouped into these categories:

1. Ignorance, stupor, laziness, dullness, narrow-mindedness, etc.
2. Clinging, desire, longing, addiction, etc.
3. Aversion, aggression, fear, hatred, worry, etc.
4. Pride, ego inflation (a subcategory of no. 3)
5. Jealousy, competitiveness (also a subcategory of no. 3)

When we speak of the *Three Poisons*, we're to understand that no. 4 and no. 5 are subsumed under no. 3.

Five Primordial Yeshes: The first division into multiplicity, emanating from the unified nature of the Dharmakaya. Yeshe divides into its five basic aspects, like facets of one jewel. This is on the Sambhogakaya level. Each of the Five Poisons, without its adventitious, deluded element—in other words, in its pure essence—is one of the Five Primordial Yeshes. Below they are listed in the order in which the Five Poisons were listed:

1. Yeshe of Basic Space
2. Discerning Yeshe
3. Mirrorlike Yeshe
4. Equalizing Yeshe
5. All-Accomplishing Yeshe

Four Boundless Qualities: Loving Kindness, Compassion, Sympathetic Joy, and Equanimity. They are four avenues we can follow, to come to the truth of our deep, loving connection to each and all beings.

Four Thoughts: The longer term is "Four Thoughts That Turn the Mind (from Samsara)." This is a group of four contemplations that, from four different entry points, guide us in a thorough exploration of our larger situation within Samsara.

Karma (Sanskrit; "action"): In this context it refers not only to actions but to their natural consequential effects. Think "Ye shall reap what ye sow."

Lama (Tibetan): A title equivalent to *rabbi* or *minister*. In Vajrayana the lama is often more of a spiritual mentor than their Christian counterpart or than in Theravada Buddhism.

Mahayana (Sanskrit; "Great Vehicle"): That branch of Buddhism which has the Two Purposes as motivating factors: enlightenment for self *and* for others. In every school of Mahayana Buddhism, one takes a vow to help *all* beings toward enlightenment.

Mala: A garland of beads used by Buddhists, and those of other spiritual traditions, to track repetitions during prayer or meditation.

Marigpa (Tibetan): Lack of awareness. Usually translated as "ignorance."

Merit: Positive effects of actions, in particular. Like an entry appearing in the credit column of the karmic "ledger."

Mindstream (Tibetan: *gyüd*): That very subtle thread of consciousness that flows from moment to moment, incarnation to incarnation. It's that fleck of awareness that identifies itself as "I" in sentient beings. When we say that one wave went up, down, and up again, it isn't the same shape, nor does it have the same molecules in it, yet there's some kind of momentum that we have in mind, in calling it the same wave. Mindstream is like that.

Ngöndro [NGÖN-dro] (Tibetan; "Preliminary Practices"): These are practiced after Shiney and before more advanced practices. Actually, Ngöndro is incorporated into the beginning of advanced practices too—hence the name.

Nirmanakaya (Sanskrit; "Emanation Body"): The manifestation level/aspect of shining forth from the Dharmakaya/Buddhahood. Another, further order of complexity of form, as compared with the Sambhogakaya. Perceptible to sentient beings in a warped and confused way, depending on their own karmically and habitually distorted "lens."

Original Purity (Tibetan: *kadak*): An intrinsic quality of the Dharmakaya, and all that issues from it. This, of course, includes human beings.

Relative Truth (Tibetan: *kün dzop denba*): The reality perceived by sentient beings, in their deluded state. *See also* Two Truths.

Rinpoche [RIN-po-chey]: An honorific term used for high lamas—higher than the Christian term *reverend*, but lower than *His Holiness*. Most lamas are not referred to by this title, only the most accomplished.

Root Lama: Root guru. An individual spiritual guide and mentor. This is arguably the most intimate and karmically significant of human relationships.

Sambhogakaya (Sanskrit; literally "Body of Complete Enjoyment"): The first level/aspect of spontaneous shining forth into form, from the Dharmakaya. Similar to the archetypal level of being that Jungians speak of. Rarely directly perceptible to human beings.

Samsara (Sanskrit): The cycle of existence—of birth, death, and rebirth—in which all sentient beings find ourselves. We are propelled from one situation to the next by our own deluded thoughts, negative emotions, karma, and habits of mind, from which we perform actions that, in turn, create further karmic consequences. We then react to these, mentally, emotionally, and physically. These in turn create ceaseless experiences in existence, like a self-perpetuating dream, until we finally wake up (and, as His Holiness the Dalai Lama says, "Better it be sooner").

Sangha (Sanskrit): The spiritual community.

Shamata (Sanskrit; "Tranquil Abiding Meditation"; Tibetan: *Shiney*): A meditation that is practiced, in similar forms, in all branches of Buddhism. It is taught to new practitioners in Vajrayana. Its endeavor is to calm the flow of thoughts while heightening mindfulness. Eventually, through this training, one can focus attention on one thing and have it stay there, in a clear, unperturbed, joyfully peaceful state.

Six Transcendent Perfections (Paramitas in Sanskrit): Generosity, Discipline, Forbearance, Joyful Effort, Concentration, and Wisdom.

Sublime Insight (Sanskrit: *Pali, Vipassana, Vipashyana*): This is usually practiced in conjunction with Tranquil Abiding, Shamata. Both of these practices are found in all branches of Buddhism. In Vajrayana they're seen as foundational and necessary, but as a means to further practices. In a commonly used analogy, Shamata and Vipassana are like the foundation of a house, which must be well established before the walls and the roof are added.

Sutra [SOO-tra]: The original teachings of the Buddha.

Tantra [TAHN-tra]: Further teachings of the Buddha, which are not studied or practiced by the Theravadins but are the mainstay of Vajrayana— Tibetan Buddhism.

Theravada [teh-ra-VA-da] (Sanskrit; "Root, or Foundational Vehicle, School of the Elders"): The foundational-level branch of Buddhism, common to all branches. Of the three main branches of teachings of the Buddha Shakyamuni, it was the first to be taught. It is based on the sutras, and does not include the tantras; the motivation for enlightenment is focused on one's own liberation from Samsara.

Three Jewels: The Buddha, the Dharma, and the Sangha—in which all Buddhists have vowed to take refuge until reaching complete enlightenment. The thought is that the combination of all three will greatly help us along the way: the Buddha because he has achieved enlightenment himself, so has proven to know the way; the Dharma because it is the instructions, or "map," that he provided us; and the Sangha, or spiritual community, as companions along the way.

Three Kayas: *See* Dharmakaya, Sambhogakaya, Nirmanakaya.

Three Poisons, a.k.a. *afflictive emotions* (Tibetan: *nyön-mong*): The Buddha (Shakyamuni) grouped the thousands of emotions like fear, worry, longing, etc., into three basic categories:

1. Ignorance, delusion, laziness, narrow-mindedness, and similar emotions
2. Desire, clinging, longing, and such
3. Aversion, aggression, hatred, dislike, fear, and such

Sometimes they are spoken of as the Five Poisons (see entry above), with the fourth and fifth categories under the third category, anger/aversion. The fourth is pride, inflation, and such, and the fifth is jealousy, competitiveness, and such. They are often subsumed under the third category because they are considered to be forms or subsets of anger/aversion.

Tonglen (Tibetan; "Sending and Receiving"): A compassion practice in which one breathes in the suffering of others and breathes out happiness toward them.

Tulku [TOOL-koo] (Tibetan; "Emanation Body"; Sanskrit: *Nirmanakaya*): An individual who has mastered their mind enough that they can control their landing in their next incarnation. The tulku system has been used in Tibet for heads of monasteries and sub-lineages to allow them to shoulder their responsibilities for many lifetimes. This is why His Holiness the Dalai Lama xiv is referred to as the fourteenth: he has been recognized and has held the Office of the Dalai Lama thirteen previous times.

Two Truths (Tibetan: *denba nyi*): The two aspects of reality, like two sides of one coin. These two aspects are called Relative Truth (*kün dzop denba*) and Absolute Truth, or Ultimate Truth (*dön-dam denba*).

Vajrayana: A branch of Mahayana, which uses many skillful means from the tantras to pursue enlightenment more efficiently. It is the branch of Buddhism generally practiced by Tibetans.

Vipassana (Tibetan: *Lhaktong*; "Sublime Insight"): Usually practiced along with Shamata/Shiney. The practice of seeing the true nature of either the object of our attention or us ourselves.

Wang, Lung: These are two kinds of transmissions that a lama gives to students, to connect and open their minds in a profound way to a particular cycle of teachings and/or practices.

Yeshe: Also called timeless awareness or (primordial) wisdom. The wisdom inherent in the Dharmakaya, which shines forth into all of its created emanations.

Yidam: Deity practice. One meditates on a particular realized being who personifies a particular aspect of wisdom—an archetypal image. It is widely practiced in Vajrayana.

Appendix B: Recommended Resources

LOJONG (SEVEN POINT MIND TRAINING)

I created a Lojong course for the Happify app that now lives on our website! namchak.org/meditation-ecourses. You can listen each day for a daily theme and a very short guided meditation. You can write it on a sticky note and put that where you'll run across it throughout the day. Lojong has been popular for at least a millennium, because who doesn't want to bridge between practice and everyday life?!

If you're wondering what to do with the 23+ hours of the day when you're not on the cushion, I highly recommend you check out Lojong, a.k.a. the Seven Point Mind Training teachings. Why? Because it takes you by the hand and shows you how you can use life's everyday challenges to further your progress. There are probably others who teach it, but I haven't experienced their teachings so I can't speak with authority on them. There are many commentaries on this classic by Chekawa Yeshe Dorje.

Traleg Kyabgon. *The Practice of Lojong: Cultivating Compassion through Training the Mind.* Boston and London: Shambhala Publications, 2007. This book is long but readable and includes some of the relevant neuroscience.

There is video of His Holiness the Dalai Lama giving a teaching on Seven Point Mind Training, available at dalailama.com/teachings/training-the-mind

Dilgo Khyentse Rinpoche. *Enlightened Courage.* Translated by Padmakara Translation Group. Ithaca, NY: Snow Lion Publications, 1993 and 2006. Dilgo Khyentse Rinpoche was one of the great scholars and practitioners of the twentieth century. He was the head of the Nyingma Lineage, historically the most populous in Vajrayana. He lived this text to the utmost. He was able to speak its true meaning in down-to-earth terms.

Pema Chödrön. *Start Where You Are.* Boston: Shambhala Publications, 2001. This is the most accessible for Westerners. My one quibble is that she refers to the maxims as "slogans," a term she got from Chögyam Trungpa Rinpoche. If you looked up the definitions of both words, it would be *maxim*, not *slogan*, that would mean "words to live by." A slogan is a phrase you use to sell a car or a political candidate. Oh well, that's a minor point. I still highly recommend this book!

Pema Chödrön offers Lojong materials in a variety of formats: books, cards, and MP3s of courses and talks she has given on this training. You could also attend one of her live teachings.

Pema Chödrön. *The Compassion Box.* Boston and London: Shambhala Publications, 2003. When in doubt, get this one. It includes the book listed above, as well as beautiful cards with a maxim on the front and her explanation on the back. There is a little stand so you can have it on your desk or in your kitchen, reminding you of your theme for the day.

Jamgon Kongtrül. *The Great Path of Awakening: The Classic Guide to Lojong, a Tibetan Buddhist Practice for Cultivating the Heart of Compassion.* Translated by Ken McCleod. Boston and London: Shambhala Publications, 2005. Jamgon Kongtrül "the Great" was among the most influential masters in the nineteenth century in Tibet. This is his commentary, beautifully translated by Ken McCleod. I turn to this one at least as much as any of the others.

Chögyam Trungpa. *Training the Mind and Cultivating Loving-Kindness.* Boston and London: Shambhala Publications,1993. My one quibble with this, again, is the use of *slogan* instead of *maxim.* Though his English was excellent, it wasn't his first language. In the case of this one word choice, perhaps it shows. Since he was Pema Chödrön's Root Lama, it's no wonder she uses the word *slogan,* despite her being American.

NEUROSCIENCE

Davidson, Richard J., and Daniel Goleman. *Altered Traits: Science Reveals How Meditation Changes Your Mind, Brain, and Body.* New York: Avery, an imprint of Penguin Random House LLC, 2017. As you might know, Richard Davidson is a neuroscientist who has worked closely with His Holiness the Dalai Lama for many years. Daniel Goleman is a psychologist who is also part of His Holiness the Dalai Lama's symposium called Mind and Life. Davidson and Goleman cover a wide array of positive effects of meditation on our whole systems, not just our brains. Some of the effects you might've guessed at, but many are surprising. I also enjoyed reading the adventures of how two avid meditators find creative ways to validate their inner experience with outer, rigorously gathered data.

Duhigg, Charles. *The Power of Habit: Why We Do What We Do in Life and Business.* New York: Random House, 2012. First, we have no idea how much we are driven around by habit. Using myriad studies, Duhigg shows us. Kind of embarrassing to see! And daunting. Fortunately he also offers studies showing how, over time and with skill, we can be more in the driver's seat. Spoiler alert: the key is *not* sheer will power. Another spoiler alert: it helps to do it with friends.

APPS & WEBSITES

People used to orient around their church community for all sorts of things. It's happening in other places more and more. Where is it happening for you? Would you like it to? Angie Thurston, Casper ter Kuile, and Sue Phillips invited 10 leaders from various communities, hosted by the Harvard Divinitiy School, to get together in various groupings to discuss how people *these days* gather in community around several topics: Community, Personal Transformation, Social Transformation, Purpose Finding, Creativity, and Accountability. I've *loved* their thoughtful writeups. To download or just read them, go to **HowWeGather.org**.

Time Out app. Would you like to take 30 seconds from your computer screen to rest your eyes and mind, and just be aware? Me too! I have this app, and you can set it for 15 minutes, 30 minutes, whatever you like. During the chosen length of time, it brings up a somewhat transparent image to subtly remind you to be aware for a moment. If you're in the middle of something and just can't pause, you can click to cancel it right away.

Nonviolent Communication videos. For guidance on how to talk out difficult things, saying what you want while being compassionate (not to mention upping your chances of success rather than a defensive reaction), you can watch a series of videos on YouTube about Nonviolent Communication. They're created by Marshall Rosenberg, the founder of Nonviolent Communication. He even uses puppets! We've trained in this at Namchak and love it. On YouTube just type in "The Basics of Nonviolent Communication 1.1".

How could I not mention **Namchak.org**? We don't want to leave you high and dry after reading this book, so we've developed all kinds of goodies to support your practice: audio and video guided meditations, e-courses, workbooks, a calendar of in-person and online events (including meditation coaching calls), Learning Circle Toolkits, and real human support for starting your own Learning Circle or work with a Meditation Buddy.

Well, now I've got to mention our Facebook, Twitter, and Instagram pages. Look for NamchakCommunity to join in with others who are also trying to wake up!

BUDDHIST WISDOM & PRACTICE BOOKS

Salzberg, Sharon. *Real Love: The Art of Mindful Connection.* Flatiron, 2017. In this book, the witty, warm, and masterful Salzberg offers a treasure trove of stories and wisdom about the challenges and inspiration of love in its myriad forms.

For other books in this series, or other books from Namchak, go to NamchakPublishing.com.

FORGIVENESS

Sharon Salzberg and Tenzin Robert Thurman. *Love Your Enemies.* Hay House, 2013. We're supposed to do whaat? Only if you want to want a light and open heart. Even if you're right! With stories, humor, good sense, and wisdom, this book explores working with enemies from four directions: The outer enemy, the inner enemy, the secret enemy, the super-secret enemy.

Cantacuzino, Marina. *The Forgiveness Project: Stories for a Vengeful Age.* London and Philadelphia: Jessica Kingsley Publishers, 2016. This is a collection of short stories, told by each person, about terrible things that have happened to them or their loved ones, and how they were able to come to peace with it. They don't always even call it forgiveness. They might not say they've fully healed. But whatever it is, each person is living a shining, unique example of moving from rage to a whole and loving life.

Luskin, Frederic. *Forgive for Good: A Proven Prescription for Health and Happiness* (HarperOne, 2003) and *Forgive for Love: The Missing Ingredient for a Healthy and Lasting Relationship* (HarperOne, 2009). I've referred to both of these books. They are based on the seven step method that he used at Stanford, in their successful study on forgiveness. *Forgive for Good* is for forgiving someone you may not see or spend much time with. That skill seems more important now than ever. *Forgive for Love* is for relationships at close range. Let's face it, we all have to be able to forgive each other sometimes, or life's going to be very difficult and lonely.

Watterson, Kathryn. *Not by the Sword: How a Cantor and His Family Transformed a Klansman.* Lincoln, NE: Bison Books, 2012. An inspiring, even astonishing, true story of forgiveness and courage. The subtitle pretty much says it all: a Jewish family in Lincoln, Nebraska, reaches out to a Grand Dragon of the Ku Klux Klan who has been threatening them. He eventually accepts their help, and they accept him into their lives, and home.

INSPIRING BIOGRAPHIES

Tutu, Desmond. *No Future Without Forgiveness.* New York: Doubleday, a division of Random House, 1999. In a gentle yet clear voice, he tells of the thousands of assaults on his humanity, both seemingly small and obviously horrific, that he and so many others in South Africa suffered under Apartheid. He found his way to forgiveness and healing, leading many on that path as well. In hearing his story of wisdom and heart in the face of a heartless system (and the actions that carried it out) we can't help but learn and be inspired.

Allione, Tsultrim. *Women of Wisdom.* Ithaca, NY: Snow Lion Publications, 2000. This is a revised and enlarged version of her earlier work by the same name. It's a collection of stories of female realized masters from Tibet. They are a joy to read—great weekend or pre-sleep reading!

Thich Nhat Hanh. *Old Path White Clouds: Walking in the Footsteps of the Buddha.* Berkeley: Parallax Press, 1991. Hanh was a world-famous Buddhist teacher, activist, and author of many books. In this one, he tells the story of the Buddha's life in the style of a novel, rather than a dry, scholarly account.

Appendix C: Credits & Permissions

This page is a continuation of the copyright page. Grateful acknowledgment is made for permission granted to reproduce images and to use quotes in the text.

PHOTOS & IMAGES *(Credits are for photos unless otherwise indicated)*

QUOTES

PAGE XXII: From an article by Gail Saville, "Why I Chose to Become a Jew" in Reform Judaism Magazine, Fall 1983, p. 20., and thanks to Rabbi Stuart Federow, https://www.shaarhashalom.org/meet-the-rabbi.html. See also, https://sites.google.com/site/errorsinthebible/what-jews-believe/no-original-sin

PAGE 4: "Break In The Cup" Words and Music by David Wilcox, Copyright © 1994 IRVING MUSIC, INC. and MIDNIGHT OCEAN BONFIRE MUSIC. All rights Administered by IRVING MUSIC, INC. All Rights Reserved Used by Permission. Reprinted by Permission of Hal Leonard LLC

PAGE 10: Gyatrul Rinpoche quote: Gyatrul Rinpoche (b. 1925) is a senior lama of the Palyul lineage of the Nyingma school of Tibetan Buddhism. Quoted from a friend of Gyatrul Rinpoche.

PAGE 11: David Bohm quote from *The Enfolding-Unfolding Universe: A Conversation with David Bohm* © 1978, Chapter 5 in "The Holographic Paradigm and Other Paradoxes," by Ken Wilbur © 1982. Reprinted by arrangement with Shambhala Publications, Inc., Boulder, CO. www.shambhala.com.

PAGE 13: Dalai Lama Quote: Quote attributed to His Holiness the 14th Dalai Lama

PAGE 21: Quote courtesy of the Tergar Sangha

PAGES 28, 33, & 63: Neem Karoli Baba quote: "Never throw anyone out of your heart," approved for use 3/26/2020 by Raghu @ramdass.org.

PAGE 29: *Words of My Perfect Teacher: A Complete Translation of a Classic Introduction to Tibetan Buddhism* (Sacred Literature) Paperback by Patrul Rinpoche (Author), Dalai Lama (Author); © 2010 Yale University Press. Reprinted by permission of Yale University Press. Unauthorized reproduction prohibited

PAGE 31: Reprinted by arrangement with The Heirs to the Estate of Martin Luther King Jr. c/o The Writers House as agent for the proprietor. New York, N.Y. *Strength to Love* Copyright © 1963 by Dr. Martin Luther King, Jr. Renewed © 1991 by Coretta Scott King

PAGE 34: Reprinted by arrangement with The Heirs to the Estate of Martin Luther King Jr. c/o The Writers House as agent for the proprietor. New York, N.Y. *Strength to Love* Copyright © 1963 by Dr. Martin Luther King, Jr. Renewed © 1991 by Coretta Scott King

PAGE 36: Johns Hopkins Medicine. "Forgiveness: Your Health Depends on It." Retrieved from https://www.hopkinsmedicine.org/health/wellness-and-prevention/forgiveness-your-health-depends-on-it on Feb. 21, 2022.

PAGE 36: "Granting Forgiveness or Harboring Grudges: Implications for Emotion, Physiology, and Health": Charlotte van Oyen Witvliet, Thomas E. Ludwig, Kelly L. Vander Laan; Psychological Science: Volume 12; Issue 2; pp. 117–123 © 2001; Reprinted by permission of SAGE Publications

PAGE 44: Dahl, C.J., Wilson-Mendenhall, C. D. & Davidson, R. J. The plasticity of well-being: A training-based framework for the cultivation of human flourishing. Proc. Natl. Acad. Sci. 117, 32197–32206 (2020)

PAGE 45: Luskin, Fred. *Forgive for Love: The Missing Ingredient for a Healthy and Lasting Relationship* (New York: HarperColllins 2009) pp. 32–33

PAGE 50: Pollay, David J. *The Law of the Garbage Truck: How to Stop People from Dumping on You.* © 2010 David J. Pollay. New York: Sterling Publishing Co., Inc. 2012.

PAGE 69: Copyright © Chambers Harrap Publishers Ltd 2014; Reproduced by permission of John Murray Learning, a division of Hodder and Stoughton Limited

PAGE 72: "She's Leaving Home" Words and Music by John Lennon and Paul McCartney Copyright © 1967 Sony Music Publishing (US) LLC Copyright Renewed. All Rights Administered by Sony Music Publishing (US) LLC. International Copyright Secured All Rights Reserved.Reprinted by permission of Hal Leonard LLC.

PAGE 89: Poem, "At The Pond." From *Evidence* by Mary Oliver, Published by Beacon Press. Boston. Copyright © 2009 by Mary Oliver. Reprinted by permission of The Charlotte Sheedy Literary Agency Inc.

PAGE 90: Frank Rand quote: from Alexander Wolcott radio show 1933

Index

A

Absolute Truth, 121, 130
Academy for the Love of Learning, 149
acceptance, 12
acupressure, 76–77
affection, 20
Afflictive Emotions, 79
Alcoholics Anonymous, 12, 39, 54
American-centric news, 17
anger, 36, 98
anterior cingulate cortex, 136–37
Applied Buddhism, 78–80
archetypes, 49, 83, 85–87
Asanga, story of, 56–59
Atisha, 144
atoms, 118
Attachment, 73
attraction, 67
aversion, 67–68
awakening, 143
awareness, 4–5, 129, 131

B

Baba, Neem Karoli, 28, 33, 63
Bardo, 59
Beck, Martha, 85
behaving well, 32–33
blind faith, 105
Bodhicitta: Buddha qualities cultivated
  by, 5; cultivating of, 6; definition of, 3;
  motivation, 8, 21, 142; training in, 59
Bodhisattva Matraiya, 57
Bohm, David, 10–12, 15, 47, 118, 151
Bokar Rinpoche, 44, 131
Borg, Björn, 8
Boundless Compassion, 5–7, 53–60, 69
Boundless Equanimity, 15–21; definition
  of, 8, 16; description of, 6–7; practice of,
  19–20; reincarnation, 16–17
Boundless Loving Kindness, 23–29; of
  Dalai Lama XIV, 13; description of, 6–7;
  practice of, 24–29
Boundless Sympathetic Joy, 6–7, 61–63
brain: anterior cingulate cortex of, 136–37;
  functions of, 44, 136; hippocampus of,
  136; mindfulness effects on, 136–37;
  studies of, 132–34
"Break in the Cup," 4

Buddha: definition of, 47, 79, 86;
  Devadatta and, 17; hate and, 28; Heart
  Sutra, 131; planes of existence, 27;
  Sanskrit definition of, xxi, 3; teachings
  of, 55
Buddha Maitreya, 56, 58–59
Buddha Nature, 5–6, 25, 59, 66, 154–55
Buddhism: efficiency of, 83; pairs in, 5–6;
  Tibetan, xxii, xxv, 83; Tonglen in, xxv;
  Vajrayana, 59, 154–55; Yanas of, 152

C

caring, 6, 20
Chagdud Tulku, 100
Chögyam Trungpa Rinpoche, 105
Christakis, Nicholas, 150
chronic anger, 36
clearing away flaws, xxii
clearing away obscurations, 5–6, 59
Clearing the Stale Energies, xvi-xvii
clinginess, 73, 156
cognizant abiding, 134
"coherent light," 160
Compassion, xxiii, xxv; Boundless, 5–7,
  53–63, 69; definition of, 69; empathy
  versus, 69–70; Equanimity and, 69;
  Far Enemy of, 74–75; Near Enemy of,
  74–75; practice with, 21; warmth of, 4
Concentration, Transcendent, 104
Conditional Love, 73
Congleton, Christina, 136–37
*Connected: The Surprising Power of Our Social
  Networks and How They Shape Our Lives—
  How Your Friends' Friends' Friends Affect
  Everything You Feel, Think, and Do,* 150
connection, 6, 19–20, 78
consciousness, 121
constructive feedback, 49
contemplative science, 137
cortisol, 37
cravings, habit-motivated, xxii
Cruelty, 74
crying, 54
curiosity, 4

D

dak-nang, 86
Dalai Lama, XIV, His Holiness: Boundless
  Loving Kindness of, 13; foreword
  by, xi; photograph of, x; self-love by
  Westerners, 23–24

Lama Sangak Yeshe Tsomo

CURRICULUM VITAE

Education & Professional Training

2006–present: One to two months' retreat annually, with instruction and guidance from Tulku Sangak Rinpoche and Khen Rinpoche.

1995–present: Scores of teachings, empowerments, and pilgrimages, including the following:

- One-week and two-week Dark retreat instruction retreats with Tulku Sangak Rinpoche and Khen Rinpoche (2017–present).
- Semiannual ten-day Dzogchen instruction retreats with Tulku Sangak Rinpoche (2006–2010).
- Six years of ten-day instruction retreats on *The Treasury of Precious Qualities,* a classic text that includes the entire Buddhist path. Tulku Sangak Rinpoche, Khen Rinpoche, and Anam Thubten Rinpoche, instructors.
- Finished Ngöndro (Preliminary Practices). This involved 108,000 prostrations, 108,000 repetitions of the 100–Syllable Mantra, 1,200,000 recitations of the Vajra Guru Mantra, and other similarly extensive practices.
- Small-group meeting with His Holiness the Dalai Lama. Ann Arbor, Michigan (April 2008).
- Tenshuk offering to His Holiness the Dalai Lama. Dharamsala, India (as part of a ten-day pilgrimage, July 2007).
- Two interviews with His Holiness the Dalai Lama.

2005 in Nepal and 2006 in the US: Lama ordination (bestowed by Tulku Sangak Rinpoche).

1995–2005: Ongoing intensive lama training in the Nyingma tradition, with Rinpoche. The following were among the components of the training:

- Thirty 1– to 2–week training intensives.
- Traditional three-year retreat, in strict, solitary retreat conditions, under Rinpoche's direct supervision, progressing from one stage of training to the next, finishing with the highest levels of Dzogchen practice. The practice retreats were usually done three months at a time.
- Several months of study and training at Rinpoche's monastery in Nepal.
- Ongoing scholarly and spiritual study of numerous classic Vajrayana Buddhist texts.
- Increased responsibility as a teacher under Rinpoche's guidance.
- Learned to speak fluent Tibetan, allowing ability to chant in Tibetan while understanding the meaning, to act as translator for students and practitioners, and perhaps most important, to speak extensively with Rinpoche and Khen Rinpoche, as well as other lamas, about the Dharma.

1990: MA, Counseling Psychology, Antioch University (emphasis: Jungian studies).

1987: BA, Counseling Psychology, Antioch University.

Affiliations & Memberships

Namchak Foundation, Montana. Co-founder, current board member.

Academy for the Love of Learning, Santa Fe, New Mexico. Founding Board member.

Ewam (US and international nonprofit center and school). Founding board member, board member, 1999–2004.

Light of Berotsana translation group, Boulder, Colorado. Board member, 2002–2008.

Namchak Foundation (US and international group with physical and online presence, dedicated to supporting people of the Namchak Lineage in Tibet and developing retreat sites). Co-founder with Namchak Dorlop Dorje Lopön Choeji Lodoe.

Pleasant Ridge Waldorf School, Viroqua, Wisconsin. Founder and board member, ca. 1975.

Selected Publications

The Dharma of Dogs: Our Best Friends as Spiritual Teachers, edited by Tami Simon. Sounds True, 2017. "Lama Kusung," pp. 33–35.

Why Is the Dalai Lama Always Smiling? (the earlier incarnation of Book 1: *Why Bother?* and Book 2: *Wisdom & Compassion*). Namchak Publishing, 2016.

The Lotus and the Rose: Conversations Between Tibetan Buddhism and Mystical Christianity, with the Reverend Dr. Matthew Fox, Namchak Publishing, 2018.

"Ani Tsering Wangmo: A Life of Merit" in *Lion's Roar Newsletter*, March 2010. "Coming Home" in *Originally Blessed*. Oakland, CA: Creation Spirituality Communities, 2008.

"Dharmasala" in *Lion's Roar Newsletter,* August 2007.

"Shedra" in *Lion's Roar Newsletter*, February 2006.

Selected Presentations & Teachings

"From Inner to Outer Work," plenary session, Lions Roar ReAwaken Summit. 2020.

"Our Watershed Moment: Inner and Outer Work for Engagement," SF Dharma Collective. 2020.

"Deepening Our Feeling of 'Us'," plenary session, Science and Nonduality Conference. 2019.

"Expanding Capacities for Joy and Connection: Science and Practice," plenary session with Richard Davidson, PhD, and Lama Tsomo, Greater Good Science Center "Science of Happiness" Conference.

A variety of teachings, including weekly and short retreats (2005–present) when on-site at the Ewam center and at other US and international sites, including the New School in New York, Spirit Rock in California, East Bay Meditation Center, etc.

"Building the 'We' Economy from the Inside Out," cocap 2019. Solo talk on compassion, then plenary session with Angel Kyodo Williams, Reverend Deborah Johnson, Konda Mason, and others.

Book launch events for *The Lotus and The Rose,* including "An Evening with Lama Tsomo and Matthew Fox," Sacred Stream, Berkeley, California; "East Meets West at Grace Cathedral," San Francisco.

Book launch events for *Why Is the Dalai Lama Always Smiling?* including "A Conversation with Van Jones," New York City; "A Conversation with Lama Tsomo and Sharon Salzberg," New York City; "Google Talks with Lama Tsomo," Mountain View, California.

Multiple co-presentations, including weekend retreats/workshops with Aaron Stern, founder of the Academy for the Love of Learning, and with Khen Rinpoche.

Three-hour introduction to Tibetan Buddhism, shown on TV in Taiwan. This was posted on YouTube in five installments.

Two guest appearances at the University of Montana School of Social Work. 2011.

"Once Existing from Self, Your Life Target Will Come Out Like Art Creation" (presentation to educators, students, artists, and general public). Miaolie Pottery. Miaolie, Taiwan. May 2010.

"Solving Confusion in the Mind" (presentation to Taiwan Sunshine Women's Association). Taichung Ewam Centre. Taichung, Taiwan. May 2010.

"Experience Sharing: To Change Your Life and Career from Miserable to Successful by Learning the Methods of Mind Observation Training" (talk to twenty-five business owners and senior managers). Howard Hotel. Taipei, Taiwan. April 2010.

"Learning Buddhism" retreat. Taichung Ewam Centre. Taichung, Taiwan. April 2010.

"Learning Buddhism and Doing Practices to Clarify Confusion." Howard Hotel. Taipei, Taiwan. April 2010.

"Seven Point Mind Training." Yung Ho Training Centre. Taiwan. March 2010. "Seven Point Mind Training, 3rd Installment," retreat. Ewam. Arlee, Montana. November 2009.

"Inner Peace/Outer Peace: What Is the Relationship?" (with Frances Moore Lappé). Peace Festival. Ewam. Arlee, Montana. September 2009.

"Seven Point Mind Training, 1st Installment," retreat. Ewam. Arlee, Montana. April 2009.

"Seven Point Mind Training, 2nd Installment," retreat. Ewam. Arlee, Montana. May 2009.

"Organic Food and Buddhism" (presentation to second-level Buddhists). Howard Hotel. Taipei, Taiwan. March 2009.

"Skillful Means Using Dharma to Benefit Others in Our Daily Lives." Ewam Center. Hong Kong. March 2008.

"Interaction and Modification of the Buddha Dharma Internal Spirit." Haufan University. Taipei, Taiwan. March 2008.

"Transforming Inner and Outer Worlds: Christian Mysticism and Tibetan Buddhism" (presentation with the Reverend Dr. Matthew Fox). Jung Center of Houston. February 2008.

"East Meets West: Christian Mysticism and Tibetan Buddhism" (presentation with the Reverend Dr. Matthew Fox). Stanford University Continuing Studies. Palo Alto, California. June 2007.

"Skills to Face Suffering" (Tonglen or Tranquil Abiding presentation to cancer patients). Tuen Mun Hospital. Hong Kong. January 2007.

"A Journey to a Peaceful Mind" (presentation to social workers and clients). City Hall Conference Room. Hong Kong. January 2007.

"How to Handle Suffering" (presentation to nursing staff). Tuen Mun Hospital. Hong Kong. January 2007.

"The Lotus and the Cross/The Lotus and the Rose" (invitation-only dialogue with the Reverend Dr. Matthew Fox). Academy for the Love of Learning. Location: Upaya Zen Center. Santa Fe, New Mexico.. November 2006.

Series of interviews and presentations on Life TV, Taiwan (a 24–hour nationwide TV station devoted to Buddhist teachings). Topics included "The Pursuit of Happiness" (part of Woman Psychology Seminars). December 2006.

"Introduction to Buddhism and Buddhist Practice" (thirty-hour intensive course). University of Creation Spirituality. San Francisco, California. 2005.

Buddhist retreat (leader) on Ngöndro. Academy for the Love of Learning. Santa Fe, New Mexico. Location: Upaya Zen Center. Santa Fe, New Mexico. May 2005.

Select Media Appearances

"Tools of Transformation When on Lockdown: Liberation vs. Freedom," Awakin Calls with Jacques Verduin, 2020.

"Sustaining Our Spiritual Practices in the Face of Frustration and Discouragement," Awakin Calls, 2019.

"Meditating with Others," Present Moment podcast, 2019.

"Journey from Financial to Spiritual Inheritance," Untangle podcast, 2019.

"Coming Awake to Your Projections and Loving Yourself", Sounds True blog, 2019.

Metta Hour Podcast, Episode 84, 2019.

Buddha at the Gas Pump Interview, 2019.

"Why Society Needs More Love," An Interview with Van Jones and Lama Tsomo, Lion's Roar magazine, 2017.

"10% Happier with Dan Harris and Lama Tsomo," 10% Happier Podcast, 2017.

Synhrnoisity Podcast, 2016.

"Lama Tsomo : Why Is the Dalai Lama Always Smiling," The Secular Buddhist Podcast, 2016.

"Buddhist teacher expands Tibetan tradition in Montana," Missoulian, 2016.

"Lama Tsomo: Finding the Ocean of Joy: Tibetan Buddhist Practice for Westerners," Insights At the Edge with Tami Simon, 2016.

Lama Tsomo walking with Tulku Sangak Rinpoche

Acknowledgments

It seems only right to begin with my family. My parents permanently infected me with the joy of exploring the nature of reality and understanding people. During my growing-up years, my sister sat with me for hours as we passionately replicated that pursuit. She's the real writer in the family, not to mention a brilliant editor, and she's always graciously encouraged my efforts.

I also want to thank Herman Schaalman, my family's rabbi, who gave me my first guidance and pointed me in the right direction in my pursuit of wisdom and compassion.

Four more whom I wish to acknowledge are my dogs Gonpo, Soongma, Kusung, and Dawa, my loving companions over the many years of writing this book . . . well, except for one writing stint at the monastery in Nepal. I deeply regretted that they were too big to fit in my carry-on bag.

They say that everyone needs a witness our lives. Aaron Stern is that for me. And so much more. We've been deep thought partners on many subjects, always learn from each other, and are closer than many brothers and sisters. So his presence permeates this book in ineffable ways.

I'm a teacher, and this series is a succession of many teachings. If it weren't for all of the students over the years and decades, I would not know what or how to teach. If it weren't for students' needs calling this forth from me, I wouldn't have troubled myself to write it. If it weren't for future students, I certainly wouldn't have written it. For all of this, and their inspiring open-minded and open-heartedness, I'm deeply grateful.

I feel a great deal of gratitude for my editor, the late Michael Frisbie, who was not only top-notch at the art of editing, but a natural and accomplished educator. Given that this was my first real attempt at a full-length book, I needed both of those gifts in great measure. Had it not been for him, this whole series would have been just a nice manual. That is what I'd originally had in mind. But because of his genuine enthusiasm for the material (despite not being a Buddhist at the start) and his skills, his questions and comments inspired the rest of this book, which was actually in there somewhere. He always gave generously, and with good humor. Actually a hysterical sense of humor! He was the patron saint of my writing for many years, and a good friend. I will miss him.

For the beautiful layout and design, applause to Kate Basart, who is not only skillful and talented but a pleasure to work with. Thanks to Kristyn Asseff for her care and skill in proofreading, and to Colleen Kane and Ellen Burke from Namchak Publishing, for holding the many threads that wove together for the final product. Many thanks to Merry Sun for her excellent editing with a Millennial take; I would have no idea!

Much gratitude to the entire Namchak team, who contributed to the many aspects of putting a book together and sending it off into the world. I'm especially thinking of Keegan in IT, for wrestling Word to the ground repeatedly, and to Mitch, for jumping in as needed. Much gratitude to Jessica Larson, director of Education and Outreach, for her many key roles in bringing this out into the world. Marissa Fornaro, at Namchak, did a masterful job at expanding our reach into the foreign-to-me world of social media. Thanks also, to the team at BerlinRosen for their expert advertising work, which they wove into our efforts.

Many thanks to Janna Glasser, not only for her excellent tracking down of the shocking number of permissions for this book, but for the various legal agreements as well. But beyond that she is one of our more ardent supporters. Gratitude to JoAnn Hogan for managing the countless details necessary for the success of this project.

Dr. Richard Davidson, one of the neuroscientists in the Mind and Life Institute working with His Holiness the Dalai Lama xiv, and head of the Center for Healthy Minds and of the Waisman Center at the University of Wisconsin–Madison, took precious time from his busy schedule to talk to me and review my neuroscience pieces.

I feel these acknowledgments must include—and highlight—the masters of the Namchak Lineage, our particular branch of the larger Nyingma Lineage, beginning with Guru Rinpoche and Nup Sangye Yeshe, who hid the teachings, then Tsasum Lingpa, who later revealed those teachings, continuing in an unbroken thread of wisdom, down to the present world lineage holder, Tulku Sangak Rinpoche, to whom this book is dedicated. He is my Root Lama. And my deep gratitude to Namchak Khen Rinpoche, Tulku Sangak Rinpoche's brother, who has also taught me much profound Dharma. Perhaps his greatest teaching is his living evidence of its efficacy.

The most recent revealer of the teachings of our lineage was Pedgyal Lingpa, who passed them directly to Tulku Sangak Rinpoche. Without every one of the lineage lamas passing the wisdom down from one to the next with utmost capability and care, I would not have received the gems that I talk about in this book. A lineage of teachings that is revealed and passed down in this way is referred to as a treasure. And that's actually an understatement.

I wouldn't want to receive all that Rinpoche and those who came before have offered me and not transmit what I can. Whenever I felt my lack of readiness too keenly, I also had this thought: if I had come upon this book when I was much younger, I know that I would have been delighted to use it for foundational learning. If this book turns out to be of benefit to you, then my purpose for writing it will have been fulfilled.

This book is the third in a series.
If you'd like us to let you know
when the next books are available,
please sign up for eNews
notifications at the Namchak
website, Namchak.org